SORTED

Published by Agapé Ministries Ireland Ltd
May 2013

Copyright © David Wilson 2013

All rights reserved. No part of this document may be reproduced or transmitted in any form or by any means, electronic, mechanical, photocopying, recording, or otherwise, without prior written permission of Agapé.

ISBN 978-0-9565814-1-9

Agapé
5 Clarinda Park North
Dun Laoghaire
Co. Dublin
www.agape.ie
office@agape.ie

Printed by
Ross Print Services, Greystones, Co. Wicklow
www.rossprint.ie

Available from:
Footprints, 87 Lower George's St.
Dun Laoghaire, Co.Dublin
dl.bookshop@scriptureunion.ie
Tel: 353 (0)1 663 8773

SORTED
david wilson

To Pam: my friend, wife and
adventurous companion in following Christ

ACKNOWLEDGEMENTS

Cover image © Getty images. Used with permission.
The Times / NI Syndication, (2000) © Nigel Williamson.
Used with permission.
The Irish Times 2012 © Used with permission
Vox Magazine 2012 © Used with permission

All Scripture quotations, unless otherwise indicated,
are taken from The Holy Bible, New International Version®
(Anglicised), NIV®.
Copyright © 1979, 1984, 2011 Biblica, Inc.
Used by permission of Hodder & Stoughton Limited,
a division of Hachette UK. All rights reserved worldwide.
'New International Version' and 'NIV' are registered
trademarks of Biblica, Inc. Used by permission.

CONTENTS

	Foreword	xi
	Preface Sorted	1
1.	Destiny	3
2.	Impact of forgiveness	15
3.	Deep breath	31
4.	Walking – fresh and balanced	45
5.	Walking through war, by faith	61
6.	Recommendation	71
7.	Taking the initiative	87
8.	Worldwide net	99
9.	Leadership	119
10.	Tooled up	131
	Study guide	137

FOREWORD

It is most surely in the interests of all human beings to have an understanding of who, what and why we are. Furthermore it is imperative that this understanding is an informed one - one to live by.

The world is full of uninformed opinions. Notwithstanding many good and noble human endeavours and achievements, much of the world is in a state of chaos. There is much fear, conflict and an immense amount of suffering amongst so many.

Religion – man's futile attempts to discover God – has been more trouble than help. Christianity is not a religion, it is a relationship – a restored relationship with God through the historical Jesus.

This most refreshing little book is a warm, sympathetic guide and handbook to take us through to this restored relationship, and urges us, as we are compelled to do, to pass on to the whole of mankind the greatest news ever. Years of valuable experience show in its approachable style. It brings back old memories for me of my first contacts with Campus Crusade for Christ/Agapé!

Here you will find a good guide for new young Christians or for those who are coming back to faith after perhaps departing for a time.

Teran Synge
Dublin
May 2013

SORTED

This book is designed to help all of us get a grip on what we believe, in vocabulary that normal people expect from a daily newspaper.

For me it started early. I watched in amazement as children of my acquaintance (mostly girls, as I recollect) burst into tears after coming to Christian faith in our Mission Hall in Strabane, County Tyrone, where I grew up. (I was relieved to find out, much later, that girls can cry when they're happy and that they can cry and laugh at the same time.) My wonderment was about what exactly went on in a person when they trusted themselves to Christ.

For others, who don't quite remember why they can be sure of their status with God, a wobbly journey begins where they get worried sick about committing the 'unpardonable sin.' If not unpardonable, it was certainly unmentionable as nobody in church meetings seems to talk about the pickle they're in. Some are stuck in a rut of addiction that makes any talk of personal growth a moot point.

Websites, books and seminars are offering me a bewildering array of boosters to my spiritual life. What would happen if I took none of them? While we're at it, what does God actually expect me to be getting on with now? Is there a bog standard limited menu for a plodding believer like me?

At exactly that stage in my life I ran into the work of Bill Bright of Campus Crusade for Christ who had taken the trouble of writing about the principles of the Christian life in a style that was, for me, digestible. This took such a load off my mind that I determined that if I ever got the chance I would like to pass on those same ideas in a way that was comprehensible to a new generation – and here it is! Many of the staff of Agapé had a hand in the formation of this book – I am grateful to each of them. Kelly Mulholland and Matthew Broderick designed the guide for group discussion or personal study.

Fuzzy talk makes for fuzzy thinking. And that only fosters doubt about salvation, and nervousness about letting on to anybody that you believe all this – let alone trying to get people to join you!

It doesn't have to be this way! It's time to get clear about the things that are worth getting clear about. There are enough mysteries in life already. Let's get the big things 'sorted'.

… CHAPTER 1

DESTINY

Commanding attention

"Jesus of Nazareth has been the dominant figure in the history of Western culture for almost twenty centuries," says Jaroslav Pelikan, History Professor at Yale University.

> "If it were possible, with some sort of super-magnet, to pull up out of that history every scrap of metal bearing at least a trace of his name, how much would be left? It is from his birth that most of the human race dates its calendars, it is by his name that millions curse and in his name that millions pray. 'Jesus Christ is the same yesterday and today and forever.' (Hebrews 13:8)"[1]

In *Beyond Consolation* John Waters says that after "growing up in the Ireland of the 1960s" he felt

> "anger at the abuses I perceived in the administration of Christianity in my own culture...It strikes me now that I never once attached any of the anger I felt towards the person of Jesus, never once had a negative thought about Him, never once felt that I should blame Him for anything. This is interesting, because I don't think I am alone in this. Strangely, although our modern, once Christian cultures have turned their backs on Jesus, they have never actually rejected Him."

He observes that most voices in our cultures, "Do not, as a rule, attack the person of Christ, or suggest that He is not who He claimed to be."[2]

Adventure

Knowing Christ is the greatest adventure a person can experience. It involves finding out how we fit into his grand scheme of things and the unique role he has for us in making an impact together on the world around us. In the Gospel of John Jesus said of his

---

[1] J. Pelikan *Jesus Through the Centuries* (New Haven, London: Yale University Press, 2000), 1

[2] J. Waters *Beyond Consolation* (London: Continuum, 2010), 208

disciples, "I have come that they might have life, and have it to the full."³ For this expression "to the full" he chose a word which means "full and overflowing". So Jesus does a lot more than just meet our needs. You hear people talk about Jesus that way sometimes: you have a headache – take aspirin; you have a problem – take Jesus. In fact that is only the beginning of what he is capable of.

He deliberately gives us 'too much' life. Now why would he do a thing like that? Because, starting with you, he would like to spread the 'extra' throughout the unique set of relationships you inhabit. As you share God's love with those he has put in your path you will become not just unforgettable to them, but you will have the privilege of bringing friends to eternity. John again, in his first letter, says, "The one who does the will of God becomes part of the permanent."⁴ Have you yearned for your life to count for something? Who hasn't? But when, at the end, the Lord comes to review our lives, those that stand out as "part of the permanent" will not be distinguished as politicians, stars of stage and screen, thinkers, wealthy or religious, but those who did the will of God.

Significant life

When I travel on the London Underground it never fails to amaze me how many adverts assume the readers are unhappy with their jobs. They are offered opportunities to look better at work, something to read on the way there to take their minds off what lies ahead, opportunities to smell better, food to cook super-fast when they come home at night exhausted, music to listen to thereafter, extreme sports for the holidays, air-conditioning for the office, relocation to Scotland, a trip to Scotland for the weekend anyway and always, always – how to find a different job. The DART in Dublin is no different. The pictures tell the

---

3   John 10:10

4   1 John 2:17, trans J.B. Phillips

same story – your body is in the office but your mind is in Eilat, Turkey, Florida, the Bahamas, wherever. And what's more, you'll need travel insurance for that. And while you're at it, try and stop smoking. Not exactly the story of people who feel the weight of their destiny in life!

Imagine a life where there were significant things to do, not just after work, but at work and throughout the work itself. Imagine getting up in the morning knowing full well that today will contribute to your calling in life, whether you work from home, at school or in a factory canning baked beans. What enterprise offers such a feeling of destiny? Actually, there is one ready for you as soon as you're ready for it!

Under starter's orders

That's because Jesus of Nazareth offered a destiny – not only in the next life but in this one. Before he left for heaven he gathered his disciples around him and gave them a little talk they were never going to forget. Even those of them who were to live to the end of that century spent their whole lives in the light of the words Christ spoke on that day. Others gave their lives in carrying out these instructions which he laid out for them: "All authority in heaven and on earth has been given to me. Therefore go and make disciples of all nations, baptising them in the name of the Father and of the Son and of the Holy Spirit, and teaching them to obey everything I have commanded you. And surely I am with you always, to the end of the world."[5]

These eleven men had spent the previous three years watching Jesus as closely as you can ever watch another person. They saw the strength of his character in the unguarded moments. They saw him break down and cry over the fate of local people who had chosen to pick a fight with God. They saw him display awesome power over nature in public and they watched him salvage the hopeless in private.

---
5 Matthew 28:18-20

What had started as a sneaking suspicion had time to give way to a huge fact – here in their own backyard they were dealing with the Son of the living God. Or rather, he was dealing with them. His patience was such that he took all the time in the world to teach them what was going on. His teaching wasn't at all like the usual religious fare. It had a definiteness that showed he knew what he was talking about and a personal ring about it through which his own character leaked out. If you had read the Scriptures (and some of them had) you would soon recognise that this was the character of God himself. It was now obvious that when God wanted to interrupt history he sent a Person, not an e-mail. It was a matter of seeing God's love functioning, not just picking up his information.

As the disciples' respect for Jesus grew, the opinion of others in town seemed to swing the other way. This puzzle gave way to bewilderment when, during one fateful week, it looked like Jesus lost it all by getting arrested (over nothing at all), and sentenced (illegally in the middle of the night) and then the very next day (no appeal courts), executed. Just like that.

Crash course

By the end of that weekend they had had a crash course in 'there's more to Jesus than meets the eye.' He came back to life (a bit of an understatement for what he actually did!) and they had six weeks of never knowing where he was going to turn up next. Later they took notes. He had appeared morning, noon and night – literally. One morning he cooked them a grilled fish and brown bread breakfast. Yes, he was physically there okay but he was also in a new dimension and he spent most of that month of April, and beyond, talking to them about the future. You can imagine that by now he had their attention! And they had a certain fascination about what indeed he was going to do about the future. They didn't like the world the way they saw it and looked forward to him sorting it out.

But the hair stood up on the back of their necks one day when he said that this was it, goodbye, and yes, there would be a great future but they were the ones who would take on the shaping of it, not him personally. He said that this would be the purpose of the rest of their lives, and not to worry their heads about how to manage all this because he was transferring power to them. As he left to go to heaven (directly!) his power was so dazzling it took two angels to persuade them to move off square one – they were standing staring up into the sky. They had wondered if this adventure would never end. Now apparently it had just begun. They all trooped back into town to wait for the next instalment.

Doing anything this century?

You can be part of that same endeavour as it continues today. Here's a venture with openings for anyone. You will find that something deep down inside you is satisfied by carrying out your Saviour, Friend and Captain's wishes. Christ will infuse your life with meaning because it will all add up to something significant. And when he gave that ongoing instruction to "make disciples" he wasn't just talking about multiplying adherents to the Christian faith. Inherent in the marching orders was quality – the growing Christian community was to mirror the style of living he himself had taught and demonstrated. Who would turn down an adventure that promised destiny and quality?

Getting personal

Precisely because this is an adventure and not just a picnic I need to ask you a rather personal question before we get too far down this road. Is your own relationship with God secured? I mean, will it take the knocks that life will undoubtedly throw at it? Where are you at in your spiritual pilgrimage right now? Maybe you have drifted into a circle of Christian friends. May I commend you – they can be great fun. Maybe you have had a definite spiritual experience that has changed your whole perspective. Maybe, like me, you had a good Christian background (don't knock it). But wouldn't you like some kind of objective proof that you are right with God and that he will happily recognise you as his child when one day you turn up to meet him? I know what that feels like. I don't know about you but, to put it bluntly, I definitely wanted to be 100% sure I was going to go to heaven when I died. Nothing short of a total amnesty was going to help me.

You see, I was brought up in Strabane, County Tyrone, by my best friends – my father and mother! I say 'best friends' because not only did they teach me the Bible from before I was able to read, but the way they lived in our house showed anybody with two eyes in their head that the Bible way of life worked. You are expecting me to say "of course they had their faults" but that is something they told me themselves. It wasn't just a Bible way of life, it was a forgiven way of life and it reeked of authenticity. For that very reason I needed to check very carefully that this was all valid by external standards outside the warm cocoon of our family. Indeed, when I was a child my father said, "You're a member of the Wilson family because you were born into it and it's nice to have you in the house. However, there are two families in our house. The other one is God's family and to get into it you have to be born again." Since I had no clue as to how babies were born the first time, let alone "again," this mystified me.

When my father later asked me if I was "born again" I had to say that I had no idea about how that worked. He then set about to explain how it "worked," despite the fact that he had an excruciating stammer and what will take me a couple of lines to write took him forever to say. How thankful I am now that he took the trouble! He referred me to the end of the Bible where Christ makes his offer of a personal relationship with God one last time. There he says, "Here I am! I stand at the door and knock. If anyone hears my voice and opens the door, I will come in and eat with him and he with me."⁶ This looked like the kind of cast-iron promise that I needed and everything in the room said, "Do it." But it took me a while. I knew that this required me to get off my high horse and admit to God that I needed him badly and that I wanted to turn myself in for this amnesty. Easy to say, but it was like pulling teeth to get down to saying, "Lord Jesus, come into my life and throw the devil out of it." (That's all I could think of to say and it completely ran the gamut of my personal theological vocabulary.)

Although I knew my dad heard me, what I now needed was confirmation from some reputable source outside our family – and that he found in double-quick time. He went to the bookcase (to this day I remember its bevel-edged glass doors) and took out a big Bible, turning to the gospel by Luke. There he showed me in chapter 15 that "there is rejoicing in the presence of the angels of God over one sinner who repents." I read it over for myself. Here it was in black and white that somewhere, anywhere, outside of Strabane, they were recording my decision (and getting enormous enjoyment out of the process).

It's a good thing I didn't start out my Christian life on the basis of what other people said. Some of my parents' adult friends didn't believe me. Then, teachers at school didn't know what to make of me. A maths teacher in Strabane Grammar School eventually decided to re-name me "Daniel" because he thought my commitment would turn out to be a costly one in such a den of lions. So they called me Daniel at school for years!

Gentleman Jesus

When you think about it, the only thing that matters here is the integrity of the Gentleman who offered me salvation in the first place. He consistently taught things like, "Whoever hears my word and believes him who sent me has eternal life and will

---
6 Revelation 3:20

not be condemned; he has crossed over from death to life"[7]; "Whoever comes to me I will never drive away"[8]; "Come to me, all you who are weary and burdened and I will give you rest"[9]; "My sheep listen to my voice; I know them, and they follow me. I give them eternal life, and they shall never perish; no-one can snatch them out of my hand. My Father, who has given them to me, is greater than all; no-one can snatch them out of my Father's hand."[10]

I put it to you that Jesus is a gentleman on two counts. First, he will not barge his way into your life – he waits to be asked. Second, once you invite him to come into your life he is as good as his word and will keep his promise to come in. And stay.

Occasionally I meet people who want to invite Christ into their life again. Sometimes they do this a number of times "just to be sure", they say. Really? Don't you think it would be better form to take the promise of Christ seriously? If you are unsure where you stand in your relationship with him why not take this occasion to invite him for the last time to come into your life? You could say, "Jesus, I deliberately invite you to come into my life, to be my Saviour and to run my life as you see fit." Then, right away, thank him: "Thank you for coming in as you promised. Amen."

On a visit to Liverpool I met with a student in the kitchen of his hall of residence to talk about where he was going with his life. He had got to know a believer on the same corridor and, after talking through many of the issues about Jesus already mentioned in this chapter, Mark was ready to commit himself to Christ. He expressed this in a prayer very similar to the one above. Then I asked him if he knew now how he stood with God. He wasn't sure. (Maybe it's not a run-of-the-mill question in normal conversation

---

[7] John 5:24

[8] John 6:37

[9] Matthew 11:28

[10] John 10:27-29

but it helped to get us talking about this issue of getting Mark's voyage launched securely.) We read together from the first letter of John where he writes to his first-century friends, "I write these things to you who believe in the name of the Son of God so that you may know that you have eternal life."[11] When I say that we read it together I mean that I read as far as the word "may" and left it to Mark to pick up the next word, "know." He grinned. I asked if he thought God wants us to be sure about our eternal life. "It's obvious!" he said. "And another thing. I know God must have a plan for my life. It's amazing that we should meet today because I'm not even a resident in this hall – I'm just sleeping on a friend's floor!"

If you're ready for this venture of a lifetime then get sure of your relationship with God first. We can never know everything and admitting mystery (it's in the Bible) isn't admitting defeat. But it isn't clever to be unsure about the central issues. You may find yourself surrounded by religious advice which says that the search is the big thing in life and that God intends to keep us on our toes by having us grope in the dark for answers. This may make for interesting media but it doesn't measure up to the positive guarantees the Bible records for us.

And how are you feeling today?

What if you don't feel any different yet? For me, I first felt vastly relieved, since the main thing that had happened, so far, was having my name recorded in heaven as God's child. What matters is the fact that you can rely on God's reputation to do what he has pledged to do. He said, "To all who received him, to those who believed in his name, he gave the right to become children of God."[12] I take it he wasn't joking. But now he is bent on making us into what he calls an entirely "new creation".[13] You

---

11 1 John 5:13

12 John 1:12

13 2 Corinthians 5:17

can certainly expect your feelings to change since everything else is due to change anyway! But don't lean on your feelings for signs that you are accepted by God. You've got much harder evidence than that – God's own signature in the Bible.

Stepping-out time

Maybe you wonder, "But what if my faith isn't big enough?" Fair question – but what's really at issue here? Surely it's a matter of what you are putting your faith in. In the far northern countries you see people fishing in the lakes in the dead of winter by going out on the ice and cutting a hole for their fishing line. They know that the thickness of the ice is well sufficient to take their weight. (They drive lorries on it all winter too!) But on a visit to Finland I learned that the thickness of the ice is all-important. A friend showed me a lake where they "lose people every spring" because they go out fishing on ice that is too thin. "But why would they do that?" I asked. "Because they're drunk and their bravado takes over from their common sense. They think they're invincible because they have great faith. But the deciding issue is only the thickness of the ice they have the faith in!" If you have put your weight on Christ the question isn't the size of the faith. The only question is – is he up to it? And I think you know the answer to that.

So, the first step in striding out into a life of destiny is to be unashamedly confident that you are a child of God. That way you will have a rock-solid foundation beneath your feet and the stability to help others.

CHAPTER 2

IMPACT OF FORGIVENESS

Spiritual lethargy

Despite the rousing call of destiny many believers today feel unable, and not even inclined, to make an impact on the world around them. Some wonder if that is even possible. You know you believe but you can't understand why you don't have the energy to be like the standard model you read about in the New Testament. You begin to think that reports of 'victory in the Christian life' are ever so slightly hyped. Makes you wonder what kind of stuff those contemporaries of Jesus were made of. Were they mentally more focussed or something?

First-century impact

Well, being a breath of fresh air to those around us, explaining to them how they can come to know God too, isn't a bag of psychological tricks. It is allowing Christ to 'overflow' to others. That's the only way we can explain the impact the first-century Christians had on their world. Scarcely twenty years after Jesus had given his followers their commission to "Go into all the world and preach the good news,"[1] these erstwhile weaklings had arrived in Greece, a thousand miles and a thousand light years from their Palestinian home. The locals in Thessaloniki, who apparently liked their peace and quiet, complained that these men who had got people excited "all over the world have now come here".[2] OK – the world as the Greeks knew it. Which was quite a bit of the world. By the end of that decade Paul wrote to friends in Turkey to say that "all over the world this gospel is bearing fruit and growing."[3] And we're not even talking here about anywhere near the end of the first century.

The world they set out to change in that first century was multi-faith and multi-racial with a newly-developed global

---

[1] Mark 16:15

[2] Acts 17:6

[3] Colossians 1:6

communications system. Sound familiar? The citizens of that world had, for the first time, got used to the idea that they could talk to each other in a trade language (Greek). To allow themselves access to any territory in Europe, the Romans had just built a continental network of roads, many of which are still used today (you can tell they never made it to Ireland – we had to wait another 2000 years to get *some* straight roads!).

The Romans liked their religion to be tolerant so, like the Greeks, they took on a whole range of gods, some nasty, some nice. You could pick and mix the ones with which you resonated best. Everyone would be tolerant of your choice – unless you chose to claim exclusively that your god was the only one – which is what the Christians did when they proclaimed that Jesus was It. Mind you, they had the resurrection to back them up. So the Romans called the Christians 'atheists' (!) which, for them, meant that you wouldn't tolerate the range of gods.

By the second century Christians were being persecuted wholesale for their loyalty to Christ. When Polycarp, a great church leader from Smyrna (Izmir in modern Turkey), was brought to the arena to be burned they gave him one last chance to deny Christ. His response was, "Eighty-six years I have served him, and he never did me any wrong. How can I blaspheme my King who saved me?"[4] When you consider the persecution unleashed on the early believers, it is amazing that the Church got into the second century and even more amazing that she got out of it.

You will be glad to hear that God has not been caught on the hop by our cosmopolitan world. Nor has he left us in the lurch as to how we should conduct our life and witness in a pluralist world. Indeed the remarkable thing is that the first century era into which God spoke bears such similarities to our world now.

---

4 C. Richardson *Early Christian Fathers* (Philadelphia: Westminster Press, 1953), 152

Opportunities surround us

How about asking God to do in our culture what he did in theirs? He hasn't changed. We are surrounded by opportunities that previous generations haven't had. Many of the world's 'isms' have been discredited. Here I am not just thinking of political systems like communism but the irrational optimistic humanism upon which much of twentieth century thought was built. People are now seeking a basis of morality. Morality itself seems to be a new mantra in politics as political parties seem to be daring each other to reveal the basis of their moral values. In business, ethical practice has become a buzzword. Company directors are queasy about attending their own Annual General Meetings unless they can answer questions on how ethical their investments are.

We are now in a time when your story is 'in.' The last generation wanted the facts: "I only believe in what I can see." This generation wants the story, the story of how it works for you. And the new generation is marching out like lemmings to seek the spiritual. People are searching for meaning. They want to experience things outside themselves and ask the big questions. As Breda O'Brien said in the *Irish Times*: "I teach young people. They are great young people, but many of them are closer to benign agnostics with a bit of holy water thrown over them than Christians. So many of them have never really encountered the Christian message. So many of them are searching for meaning."[5]

For the people of our time there is no sweeter thing than finding meaning through friendship – and they are quick to say so and show it. Does it take a rocket scientist to work out why *Friends* became cult TV, endlessly re-playing? It has become a commonplace to look askance at the thinness of 'Facebook friendship.' As if it were being prepared by God himself, our generation has true 'friendship' as flavour of the month, *every* month.

---
5 B. O'Brien *Irish Times* May 5, 2012

If the world is there for the winning why do we feel out of steam before we even get started? Two big reasons:

A. Pedalling harder

When things begin to go adrift it is not unusual for Christians to begin to pedal harder by trying to keep all the possible rules about good behaviour that they can remember. They forget that their new life was bought for them (expensively) through Christ's death on the cross and that nothing they can do will improve on his work. In 1993 a respectable middle-American housewife turned herself in to the police after keeping a secret for 23 years. In 1970 she was the driver of the getaway car used by radical activists in a bank raid in Boston in which they killed a police officer. I heard her speak to the court (they replayed it on the news) in which she said, "My entire adult life has been one long act of contrition." Her statement reminded me of those who, once they have come into God's kingdom for free, then revert to spending a whole lifetime of trying to prove themselves – to God and anyone else who's watching.

B. Hard to believe

For some, it is simply hard to take in the idea that God, having come this far, is not about to give up on us now. It seems too good to be true that our salvation extends not only to bring us into a relationship with God but also to provide relentlessly for our needs, including our sins, until the day we go to meet him. It seems incredible that he is looking forward to that day as much as we are.

When I worked in an office in Westmoreland Street in Dublin a graduate student phoned me one day to ask if we could meet and talk – but only so long as we could meet where we weren't recognised. Since I knew this guy I thought the request was a bit odd but agreed and went off to a particular restaurant in town.

It was more expensive than I would normally go for lunch – I guessed that way no one would recognise me anyway! We hadn't got far into the first course before he told me that he couldn't bring himself to feel forgiven by God. We talked backwards and forwards about the nature of Christ's provision for us by sacrificing himself but we seemed to be getting nowhere and his face looked like a thundercloud. "I think it's what I've done that's the problem," he said. "Nothing too big for God," said I, rather too quickly. Then it all tumbled out. "I worked on an oil-rig to put myself through university and got into homosexual practice which was common on the rig. Now I'm away from it all but I still get tempted – I find myself staring at people. It just doesn't fit with being a Christian." Again I said that Christ died for all our sins – and in the area of sexual morality that includes heterosexual and homosexual sin. What's more, Christians are tempted just like everybody else: "No temptation has seized you except what is common to man. And God is faithful; he will not let you be tempted beyond what you can bear. But when you are tempted, he will also provide a way out so that you can stand up under it."[6] And Christ himself was tempted "in every way just as we are – yet without sin."[7]

I still wasn't making much of an impression on my friend's face so I quit explaining and simply asked him, "Do you feel like a second-class citizen in the kingdom of God?" "Exactly," he said, "You've got it." He went on to say that he couldn't see how he deserved to be a child of God. I had a New Testament in my pocket and we read John 1:12 slowly word for word, "to all who received him, to those who believed in his name; he gave the right to become children of God." "So what are you?" I asked. "A child of God." "And is that because of good behaviour or by right?" "By right," he replied. We paid the lunch bill and he left the restaurant with his head held high.

---

6   1 Corinthians 10:13

7   Hebrews 4:15

Three kinds of people

Thankfully we don't need to stay stuck in the pedalling-faster mode or dazed by unbelief. The Bible itself provides an explanation of what is going on. It says there are three kinds of people in the world. You were maybe expecting me to say 'two kinds' – those who know Christ and those who don't. But three are outlined by Paul in 1 Corinthians 2:14-3:3: the 'Spirit-less person,' the 'spiritual person' (you might have expected these) and then he borrows a Greek expression which he calls the 'fleshly' person.[8]

Spirit-less person

Here's somebody who may well be brilliant in terms of understanding how the world works but they haven't a clue about spiritual things because they have never invited the Spirit of Christ to come and take up residence in their life. They can't call on the resources God puts at the disposal of his own children. This person isn't a true Christian at all and "does not accept the things that come from the Spirit of God" (verse 14).

Spiritual person

This one is a believer and is making good use of the power and love of God that comes by spiritual birthright. They have the joy of obeying God from a motivation of love. They see him produce what he calls "the fruit of the Spirit" in their life – qualities like "love, joy, peace, patience, kindness, goodness, faithfulness, gentleness and self-control."[9] They see others influenced for Christ and brought into peace with God. Sounds great! Who wouldn't want to be like that?! Because Christ lives in them they have a perspective on life beyond their years or experience. Paul calls this having "the mind of Christ" (verse 16).

---

8   N.A.S.B.

9   Galatians 5:22

Fleshly person

I, for one, would feel intensely uncomfortable if the Bible left it at that – just two kinds of people – the lost and the spiritual. It wouldn't fit with what I see in real life. But in its own inimitable, disarmingly honest way, the Bible accurately describes what happens to a Christian who takes their eyes off Christ. This is not offered to us as a third way to live but it sure helps me to make sense of what I see going on – especially inside me.

The next thing you know Paul is telling his friends that, much as he would like to write to them as 'spiritual' people, he would be wasting his time because they aren't ready for that quite yet.[10] Here are people who have been converted but something's not quite right in their lifestyle. They have got bogged down in an attitude of independence from God and as a result have been squabbling about the silliest things. Note that when Paul lists what's going wrong it's not the kind of sin that would be reported in the newspaper. It's things like jealousy and quarrelling. But the result is that the 'fleshly' person ends up acting like the people next door – their distinctive style of life is lost. They are no longer an attraction for others. Maybe that's the kind of people Nietzsche meant when he said that before he became a Christian the Christians would need to look more saved.[11]

A fleshly person is going to be plagued by things like worry, guilt, negative criticism, loss of love for God and for others, and plain old selfishness. They feel defeated and fruitless. The thing is they may be trying their best, in their own energy, to be a decent Christian. Most likely they don't understand what the problem is and that's scary. When Paul talks about the same problem in Romans he says, "My own behaviour baffles me. For I find myself not doing what I really want to do but doing what I really loathe."[12] Ever felt like that? Some days are better than others but you feel like you're on a spiritual roller coaster.

---

10 1 Corinthians 3:1-3

11 F. Nietzsche *Thus Spoke Zarathustra, II. 4: The Priests*

12 Romans 7:15 trans J.B. Phillips

Clock stuck

The tragedy in being a fleshly person is not just that you feel peculiar but that you have neither peace in your head nor power in your life to be getting on with that adventure for which you were born. One of the most moving people I ever knew lived in the district where I grew up. If you were to visit the farm where she lived, as our family often did, you would have seen a young teenager, ready to spring into her life, loved by her parents and siblings. Her complexion was rather pale and she didn't leave the house much. I remember her like a heroine in a Victorian novel who is always retiring to their room in the attic. Actually she wasn't a teenager. She was, by that time, in her late twenties. When she was about twelve years old something went amiss with her hormone system and her body clock never got started. So she lived a life well protected by her family who were crazy about her, but never doing all those things that a girl wants to do.

You don't want the years, or even the months, to trickle by without seeing your life making progress in the adventure God has prepared for you, do you? But that is often the fate of the fleshly Christian. The Disney movie *Tangled* (2010) was meant for kids but I have a suspicion that the title of one of its hit songs might have been aimed at their parents: *When will my life begin?* Ever feel like that?

Provision for life

Now the good news. All this has come as no surprise to God. He has gone to great lengths to make provision for our ongoing needs in life. The Holy Spirit is ever ready to load us with the power we need at every turn. You didn't think God was going to get us this far and then let us hang, did you?!

My grandfather, Robert Myles, was one of those Irishmen who emigrated to America to try to find his fortune. He made his way up to Moville in County Donegal from where he went out on the little tender to the transatlantic steamer that sat waiting at the mouth of Lough Foyle. The records of one such passenger (not my grandfather!) tell about his dutifully saving up for his passage, buying the ticket, and then setting off to cross a rough Atlantic. He tried to calculate the number of days he would be at sea and brought some provisions for the journey, composed of crackers and cheese – all he had money left for. Day one passed pleasantly; the journey between Ireland and Iceland can be quite congenial. By day two the crackers were soft and the cheese hard. The third day saw him plain hungry. One thing he couldn't figure out was why stewards went by from time to time with plates of delicious food. Eventually in some desperation he stopped one and offered to do whatever it would take, mop decks, anything, in order to eat one of those steaks. "Do you have a ticket for your journey?" asked the steward. "Of course I do," replied our intrepid traveller. "Then didn't you know that the meals come with the ticket?"

Your ticket to eternal life, in this world and the next, comes at a cost – already paid for by Somebody Else. And Somebody Else also knew you would be needing the daily diet of forgiveness and he remembered to pay for that at the same time. Like the oxygen of life, the Spirit who comes to live within us at the moment we receive Christ is available for us to 'breathe' as days go by. But first things first, before we talk about how to 'breathe in' there are going to be things we need to 'breathe out.'

Breathing out

In his first letter the apostle John explains just how far God's provision runs: "If we confess our sins, he is faithful and just and will forgive us our sins and purify us from all unrighteousness."[13] In my last term of my last year at university somebody took the trouble to introduce me properly to the idea in this passage. By

---
13 1 John 1:9

then I had had my fill of improvement programmes. I had heard preachers tell us that we should pray more, read the Bible more, think more about the second coming of Christ, get more serious about the Church. I'm sure there was a lot to commend in what they told us. It's just that I couldn't hear them properly because a nagging noise in my head said, "I want to hear how to be forgiven for my sin before I take on more of anything!" Then a kind friend took me aside and said, "You just need to get clear about being forgiven like it says in 1 John 1:9." I read the passage and felt understood. I felt like God had caught up with me in a way that was at once both embarrassing and liberating. Liberating to the extent that I felt free for the first time to talk naturally about Christ to the students around me – with whom I had just spent four years! Embarrassing because I had been tripped up by my own uncertainty about forgiveness. This charter of freedom will repay examination of the details. Let's look at these three terms: 'confess', 'just' and 'forgive.'

'Confess'

This means 'to agree with' God about our sins. Be specific. Name those things which you know are displeasing to God. A student came to our home to ask me for advice because his life had 'plateaued.' I asked him if there was any unconfessed sin in his life. No, he couldn't think of any. Any problems with attitudes that needed to be confessed to God? Nope. Any other reason why God would feel hesitant to fill him with his Spirit? Nothing came to mind. "I suppose there is one thing, though," he said. "I've been reading some books that are maybe not the healthiest." It then turned out that he had indulged himself in a line of reading material designed to rot your soul. When I asked him if he had confessed this he said, "Well, not specifically." But 'specifically' is what this passage is asking for. Then he opted to kneel down in our front room (his idea – I hadn't even suggested it) and spell out to God the exact steps he had taken which he knew were sin. I'm sure he's had his moments thereafter but from that day on his plateau seemed to disappear and he was free to stride forward towards maturity. Don't blur the hard facts of what needs to be confessed.

If we confess our sin "he is faithful" to forgive us. The day will never come when God says, "I am fed up forgiving you. You'd think you would know better by this time. Must we go round and round like this? You have used up your forgiveness coupons long ago. I don't want to see you again for weeks." It isn't in his vocabulary to talk like that. But when you think about it, you don't necessarily expect God to be described as 'faithful.' I thought we were the ones who were supposed to be faithful? God is faithful simply because he has given his word to you and will not break it no matter what you do. You cannot make him love you any less – nor can you make him love you any more.

'Just'

God can be faithful because he is just. He is not 'letting us off' our sin as if it had slipped his mind. The letter to the Romans tells us that "The wages of sin is death"[14] and this is an expense that Jesus has already paid for us, and paid very expensively. This puts him in a position where he can discharge me from my sin and, because the price is paid, he thinks he would be unjust not to! God is not grudgingly allotting me a little bit of salvation. He is jumping at the first chance to apply his special purchase to my case. When we talk about Christ dying for my sins, just how many sins does that apply to? Those committed up until I trusted Christ? Those up until today?

The letter to the Colossians gives us the answer: "He forgave us all our sins, having cancelled the written code, with its regulations, that was against us and that stood opposed to us;

---

14 Romans 3:23

he took it away, nailing it to the cross."[15] So how many sins did Christ forgive? All of them! Even those I may commit between now and when I go to heaven? 'All' means what it says. And when you think of it, every one of my sins was in the future when Jesus was on the cross. I heard one grateful woman who had spent years working fruitlessly on religion tell how she had come to finally accept God's forgiveness: "I realised that Jesus died with my name in his head." When God forgives you he is not only being just, but he can be seen to be just.

'Forgive'

As we have seen, we are forgiven because of Christ's sacrifice for all our sins. Confessing our sins to him makes real in our daily experience what has already been done on the cross. He then goes on to say that he will "purify us from all unrighteousness." Needless to say I don't even begin to realise what sins I am not yet aware of. When the Holy Spirit brings things to mind I can confess and move on. In the meantime he is dealing with unrighteousness which I am still too blind to see. Hence the glorious ending of Psalm 23, "Surely goodness and mercy will follow me all my life." I confess what I am aware of. He makes his long-standing forgiveness current today. And mercy dogs my footsteps. He leaves nothing to chance. It's year-round cover.

As we shall shortly see, moving along in life involves confessing a wrong attitude or action when God brings it to our attention and then keeping going. What would it take to become a fleshly person again (not that you'd want to)? Again 1 John chapter 1 tells us that if we refuse to acknowledge our sins we walk in the shadows instead of in the light.[16] Not a safe place to be.

---

15 Colossians 2:13-14

16 1 John 1:8

Action points

What good would this information be to you if I didn't propose a way to get started? Let me suggest the following steps: take some time aside and:

(a) Ask the Holy Spirit to show you those things that are getting in the way of your fellowship with God.

(b) Write them down on a piece of paper. I think you'd better do this where you can have a little privacy.

(c) Write out the words of 1 John 1:9 across the list, so that it covers over the sins that you wrote down. "If we confess our sins, he is faithful and just and will forgive us our sins and purify us from all unrighteousness." There's nothing magic in writing this down but it's a great object lesson to be reminded of Christ covering our sins.

(d) Destroy the piece of paper. Burn it if you have somewhere safe to do so – or cut it up into a million pieces.

(e) Thank God enthusiastically for forgiving all your sin. Thank him that "the meals come with the ticket!" If you have a back garden go out and jump up and down in it. Or whatever it is you do on these occasions.

(f) There may have been things on your list where you have wronged other people. Now it's time to make restitution to them. Or maybe you need to phone somebody – or go and talk to them and ask for their forgiveness. Or write them a letter if they're far away. Better not to do this one by e-mail.

Losing points

A few years ago when we returned to Ireland from London where we had been living, I went through the various processes of moving. One of them was changing my UK driving licence back to the Irish one. I was told to contact the Motor Tax Office of Dublin City Council in Queen Street. The girl on the phone made it sound so simple I could scarcely believe her. I even wondered if I was through to the right office. I thought her chirpiness would surely evaporate with my next question, "What about the penalty points on my UK licence?" "You have no points showing," said she (she had apparently "brought up my details on the screen"). Amazingly, I then had the temerity to argue with her, apologetically of course, "Well I do have two points from driving a little too quickly on a Sunday morning on a visit to Birmingham, the early morning sun was in my eyes, it was in an industrial estate blah blah blah." She mercifully cut me short, "Nothing showing here – UK points don't transfer to Ireland, you're all set to go." Talk about feeling forgiven!

Don't get any notions – this anomaly between the two jurisdictions has now been resolved and that's one amnesty you can't get anymore. But I started out driving in Ireland again at zero! I felt strangely free – an unexpected reminder of what God's grace feels like.

Snow

The vista that now stretches out before you is a bit like when it snows overnight in the winter. Every step you take in the morning is on fresh ground. There is a special satisfaction about walking out into a white unspoilt world. Enjoy God's forgiveness and when he brings to your attention another issue to be dealt with confess it, and keep going in the white snow of God's grace.

If guilt should return to nag at your heels, remember the only one left with a vested interest in making you feel guilty is Satan. That is his day job. God's forgiveness is complete – "There is now no condemnation for those who are in Christ Jesus."[17] A little girl who had decided to open the door of her life to Jesus was then asked, "What would you do if Satan comes to the door tomorrow?" "I'd ask Jesus to answer the door," she replied. Good advice.

---
17 Romans 8:1

There's no reason in the wide world why we wouldn't see our whole generation infused with the news about Jesus. To be the kind of authentic agents of change our generation requires we first need to experience internal change in our own lives. That will come from the confidence you find by drawing daily from God's forgiveness.

CHAPTER 3

DEEP BREATH

Making the news

Although they had been with Jesus for three years, the disciples were not equipped to carry out his special life-assignment until they were filled with the Holy Spirit. The Lord specifically told them, "You will receive power when the Holy Spirit comes on you; and you will be my witnesses in Jerusalem [same city as today, only smaller] and in all Judea and Samaria [75% of modern Israel], and to the ends of the earth [everywhere else!]."[1] The rest is history – except for the part that's not written yet – the future. That's where you come in, because you can be a fruitful witness for Christ too, helping to continue and complete in our time what they started twenty centuries ago. And we today are just as dependent on the filling of God's Spirit as they were the day they started in Jerusalem.

Nothing doing

Of course the disciples had started off with amazingly daring plans to follow Jesus even before he went to the cross. But the bravado paled quickly when they got the measure of the task and some of the plans, hatched furtively at the dead of night, never saw the light of day. Maybe that's what it took to convince them of what Jesus had already said, "Apart from me you can do nothing."[2] In those few words the Lord summed up the kernel of the Christian life. It is not difficult – it is impossible without Christ's control from the inside. When he translated the New Testament letters, J.B. Phillips wrote in his preface,

> The great difference between present-day Christianity and that of which we read in these letters is that to us it is primarily a performance, while to them it was a real experience. We are apt to reduce the Christian religion to a code, or at best a rule of heart and life. To those men it

---

1 Acts 1:8

2 John 15:5

is quite plainly the invasion of their lives by a new quality of life altogether. They do not hesitate to describe this as Christ 'living in' them.³

Lost Contact

Every summer the work at the back of our house, which I lightheartedly used to refer to as "mowing the lawn," stubbornly reminded me that it was in fact "mowing the moss." I tried all the tricks in the book to get rid of the moss until I found a more garden-conscious friend had the answer. He had attacked the problem head-on and bought a scarifier which he was happy to lend to me. That's a handy electrical gadget that you run up and down the garden, a bit like a lawn-mower, that tears the moss out as you go along. The first time I went out to do the moss with his machine it seemed to malfunction after a while. No end of tinkering with the innards seemed to resuscitate it. I wondered what I was going to tell him. Then I discovered a solution so simple it was laughable. His garden was big and square and generous. Ours was skinny and long and the mains lead didn't go far enough so the plug had pulled out of the socket back in the kitchen. All the might of the mains electricity was at my disposal. But nothing works at all if contact with the power is broken. Jesus meant it quite literally when he said, in his last big talk with the disciples before the cross, "apart from me you can do nothing."

Big introduction

A good part of that big talk was taken up with introducing the Holy Spirit (it takes up three chapters of John's gospel). Up to this point the disciples had mostly been restricted to watching Jesus operate. But on that evening he said, "I tell you the truth, anyone who has faith in me will do what I have been doing"

---

3   J.B. Phillips *Letters to Young Churches* (London: Geoffrey Bles, 1953)

(disciples' eyes wide open); "He will do even greater things than these, because I go to the Father" (open wider); then later, "It is for your good that I am going away" (disciples' mouths open).[4] I'm not so sure they could see why it was so good for Jesus to go away. They were keen for him to stay right there! But he assured them, "Unless I go away, the Counsellor [the Holy Spirit] will not come; but if I go I will send him to you."[5] There was a little something the disciples may not have yet noticed about Jesus' life. His work had been done "in the power of the Spirit" (Luke 4: 14). Did you ever wonder why Christ didn't arrive with all the panoply of power of the second Person of the Trinity? One reason was that by living in the power of the Spirit he was inventing (for us) a new way of living. Otherwise he would be a hard act to follow. But Peter, who was there on that night and eventually got the message, encouraged his correspondents (in 1 Peter) to "follow in his steps," because it was now open to them (and to us too) to be filled with the Spirit – as the norm. His plan is to continue his mission "to seek and save the lost" through us. Our responsibility is to follow Christ; his responsibility is to make us "fishers of men" (Matthew 4:19).

Breathe in

It looks like Jesus had this talk with the disciples on a Thursday evening. A lot of water flowed under the bridge over the next couple of days but when they next saw Jesus, on Sunday night, he immediately reminded them about the coming Holy Spirit. In John we read that "he breathed on them and said, 'Receive the Holy Spirit.' "[6] Not something they were ever likely to forget, not only because of the once-in-a-lifetime occasion but because their word for 'breath' and 'spirit' was one and the same. God's Spirit was going to be the oxygen of their life. To access this object

---

4 John 14:12

5 John 16:7

6 John 20:22

lesson of spiritual breathing for ourselves let's address five key questions: Who is the Holy Spirit? Why did he come? What does it mean to be filled with the Spirit? Why are many Christians not filled with the Spirit? How then can I be filled with the Spirit?

Who is the Holy Spirit?

I could never improve on Jesus' own introduction – "I will ask the Father, and he will give you another Counsellor to be with you for ever – the Spirit of truth. The world cannot accept him, because it neither sees him nor knows him. But you know him, for he lives with you and will be in you."[7] They were to expect another – like Jesus. In recording what Jesus said, John had a choice over which Greek word he would use for 'another.' He could say 'another of the same kind' or 'another of a different kind.' He chose 'another of the same kind.'

So if we want to know about the character of the Holy Spirit we need look no further than Jesus. Say, for example, you wanted to know what the Spirit thinks of children. Well, what did Jesus think of children? He seemed to get on particularly well with children – they were hardly five minutes in his company before they wanted to jump on his lap (the disciples were less than happy with this one). What does the Holy Spirit think of men? We know well how Jesus commanded the respect of a wide range of men, from fishermen, to taxmen, to political radicals, to Bible scholars, to workers with permanent dirt under their fingernails. And what does the Spirit think of women? Throughout his life's work the Lord gave women a position in his company they had never enjoyed in society before. They were a permanent part of his travelling band and there was nothing 'token' about them. When he rose from the dead Jesus did a couple of things for women that no other rabbi would ever have conceived of. It was to a woman he first appeared in the garden. He left the reports of

---

7 John 14:16,17

his resurrection hanging on her word and reputation – in a day when a woman's testimony was scarcely acknowledged. And do you notice how she recognised him? When he used her personal name, "Mary." For the times, that was a radical step. So the Holy Spirit is utterly dependable in his character, being just like Jesus. Reading the book of Acts would have given us a clue anyway when he is called "the Spirit of Jesus".[8]

But what did Jesus mean by promising a "Counsellor"? Previously this was translated "Comforter." It makes the Holy Spirit sound like a doctor with a good bedside manner – which is no bad thing – but the original word has a bit of edge to it. It means someone who comes alongside, yes to comfort, but also to energise, to galvanise and to represent you when you need it. Like a mixture of a constant companion, an inspiring sports coach who really gets you stoked with energy, and a good lawyer.

Of course this was all still theory for those disciples at that stage because historically the Spirit first came to happily invade their lives at Pentecost, still nearly a month and a half away. Hence Jesus' statement, "He lives with you and will be in you." Thereafter all believers had the Holy Spirit within them from the moment they put their trust in Christ. In fact Paul tells us in Romans, "If anyone does not have the Spirit of Christ, he does not belong to Christ."[9] So the beautiful and shocking fact is that if you belong to Christ then the Holy Spirit is living in you right now, just as present as he was at the Sea of Galilee! How amazing to have at your fingertips the privilege of calling on the help of the third person of the Trinity, who was involved in things like the Creation and the raising of Jesus from the dead!

---

8   Acts 16:7

9   Romans 8:9

Why did he come?

He came to guide us "into all the truth...he will bring glory to me by taking from what is mine and making it known to you,"[10] as Jesus told the disciples. This involves making our characters more and more like Christ.

Popular culture often thinks of the Spirit as a pliable, genial genie. Not so with the true Spirit of God. He isn't called the Holy Spirit for nothing. He also switches on our praying ability and gives us each a special capacity to serve him. Of course we would never even get off square one without the work of the Spirit. He is responsible for our new birth[11] and he 'seals' us into our new life so we can't lose it and just having him with us is regarded in heaven as our guarantee for our inheritance there later on. They'll know you OK when you get there![12]

A major reason for the Spirit's coming is "to convict the world of guilt" (John 16:8). It's a bit of a relief, for everybody I think, that Christians aren't the ones put in charge of convicting people of their guilt! But as the Spirit guides us to those in whose lives he is working we can be bringers of good news. This does not simply mean, as is sometimes popularly supposed, that the Holy Spirit comes into action to rescue my promotional efforts when I get stuck. Rather the first emphasis is that he will testify about Christ. "And you also must testify,"[13] says Jesus. We are trotting around after the Holy Spirit trying the doors of people's hearts on which he has knocked.

So it made perfect sense, by the time they got to that normal-looking field outside Bethany weeks later, when the Lord said, "You will receive power when the Holy Spirit comes on you and you will be my witnesses" – and then left them to it. Not that he was going to leave them to their own devices – they'd already

---
10 John 16:13,14

11 John 3:5

12 Ephesians 1:13,14

13 John 15:26,27

tried that! They were going to enjoy a completely new way of living, where he worked through them from the inside out!

I think the disciples had flashbacks from time to time about all that had happened when Jesus was with them. Indeed the gospels tell us that some things only made sense to them afterwards. One of these surely must be the occasion when Jesus shouted out in the Temple, "Whoever believes in me, as the Scripture has said, streams of living water will flow from within him." John puts in an explanatory note to say, "By this he meant the Spirit, whom those who believed in him were later to receive. Up to that time the Spirit had not been given, since Jesus had not yet been glorified."[14] Now John himself, and his friends, were to become a stream of help to mankind the world over. Not exactly what he had expected that first day when he innocently rolled up at the lakeside and asked Jesus where he was staying!

What does it mean to be filled with the Holy Spirit?

After Pentecost the enterprise to go to the world took off and we often read that the believers were "filled" with the Spirit. This was an ongoing way of life they now expected. Eventually Paul writes to the Ephesians, "Be filled with the Spirit,"[15] as a plain instruction, meaning 'be powered,' 'steered by,' 'under the control of' the Spirit. This is an imperative. He's saying, "Just do it." It is not a suggestion. It is also stated in the passive sense – it is God's work to fill us. And it is continuous. He implies "Go on being filled." A bit like a mother says to a child who is walking off to school in the morning, "Mind yourself" – meaning mind yourself now, and later, and all day in fact! So we are to be filled with the Spirit on an ongoing basis.

I was helped in understanding this idea of "filling" by none

---

14 John 7:37-39

15 Ephesians 5:18

other than NASA. Have you ever seen the news footage they show to use up the time on TV before a manned rocket launch? There is often great concentration on the spacesuits. (If I were an astronaut I'd concentrate on them too!) It is only through the use of that spacesuit that anything gets done beyond the control desk. What fascinates me is that each suit is custom-made to fit the wearer – and it costs a fortune. My wife and I saw the suit made for astronaut David Scott when we visited the Smithsonian Air and Space Museum in Washington DC a couple of years ago. Scott's name is stitched into a label on the suit. Just that little visor that protects their face is made of gold film (to shield them from harmful rays) and costs thousands. Of course the whole thing is a waste of money if it is left hanging on a peg. But once the astronaut gets into it and fills it then the investment is worthwhile. It's not just that he or she fills up all the room inside the suit. They completely control how it moves and what it does. They can go outside in space and fix telescopes, go for 'walks', play golf and, like Scott, drive a car on the moon! You have been intricately made too – and made for a purpose. You have been bought expensively. And now you can have your life's design realised when you are filled with God's Spirit.

What should it be like when we are filled with the Spirit? We can expect to want God's company, to develop an appetite for the Bible and to get a kick out of obeying him. A major by-product will be experiencing the love of God. This pushes Paul over the top a bit when he writes, "I pray that you may have the power to grasp how wide and long and high and deep is the love of Christ."[16] There's nothing like the filling of the Spirit to give you the "somebody-loves you" experience. Jesus himself likened the filling of the Spirit to branches growing on a vine.[17] All they have to do to produce good fruit is hang in there! This may well have given Paul his idea for the fruit of the Spirit in

---

16 Ephesians 3:18

17 John 15:1-8

Galatians as Christ's character begins to be re-created in us in the form of "love, joy, peace, patience, kindness, goodness, faithfulness, gentleness and self-control."[18] Another type of fruit to expect is seeing other people come to Christ as a result of your recommendation.

Why are many Christians not filled with the Spirit?

Some simply do not know what's available to them. They are frustrated by mediocrity but don't know how to get God's best out of life. Others are afraid of God. They imagine that God may ask them to do something very difficult in order to prove themselves. They wonder, "What if the Holy Spirit made me do something I don't want to do?" When you think about it, this idea doesn't hold together. If one of my sons were to come and say, "Dad, I want you to know that I love and respect you," would I reply by saying, "Glad you mentioned that. Now, here's something you're going to hate but I am going to force you into doing it"? Of course not! Jesus put it this way, "Which of you fathers, if your son asks him for a fish, will give him a snake instead? Or if he asks for an egg will give him a scorpion? If you then, though you are evil, know how to give good gifts to your children, how much more will your Father in heaven give the Holy Spirit to those who ask him!"[19]

Some people, and I can understand them, are afraid because they just don't want to be weird. But who's asking you to be weird? God provides filling by his Spirit to help you to be normal! You know God loves you intensely, passionately, dearly. The last thing he wants is for you to be afraid – "There is no fear in love. But perfect love drives out fear."[20] A couple of minutes' thought about how God has shown his love for you should convince you that you have nothing to fear from him, above all people!

---

18 Galatians 5:22

19 Luke 11:11-13

20 1 John 4:18

For some it's difficult to trust God's plan for their life. Why? Do you think you can improve on his ideas? Surely he has a better plan for your life than you have yourself. In his very first address to his followers Jesus said, "Seek first his kingdom and his righteousness and all these things will be given to you as well."[21] By my calculation you can't lose on this one.

How can I be filled with the Holy Spirit?

"By faith" is the simple answer. Faith is taking God at his word. That's how we start in the Christian life and we never stop exercising our faith. Paul tells the Ephesians, "It is by grace you have been saved, through faith"[22] and then goes on to say to the Colossians, "Just as you received Christ Jesus as Lord, continue to live in him,"[23] and to the Galatians, "Did you receive the Spirit by observing the law or by believing what you heard? Are you so foolish? After beginning with the Spirit, are you now trying to attain your goal by human effort?"[24]

You do not have to beg God for what is already yours by his own arrangement. When you take money out of your bank account at a cash machine you don't have to make a special application as if this were an unusual request that was nearly too much to ask for. No, you tap in your PIN number and expect the crisp notes to come out the moment you retrieve your card. After all, it's your money!

Well, are you ready for God to fill you with his Holy Spirit? If you badly want to have him lead your life and witness you're just in time. "Those who hunger and thirst for righteousness will be filled," Jesus promised.[25] It's time to breathe in. You remember we talked about breathing out in the last chapter? Did you 'breathe out' and confess whatever was displeasing to God?

---

21 Matthew 6:33
22 Ephesians 2:8
23 Colossians 2:6
24 Galatians 3:2,3
25 Matthew 5:6

That's the kind of preparation you want to make for being filled. And be ready to commit every area of your life for him to take over. Don't be careful.

All the rooms in the house

When I was a kid my father brought me to see a very old believer who was visiting locally. Strangely enough, I don't remember him as being old but he certainly was animated and just brim-full with the life of Christ in a way I hadn't seen in many others. On the way home I asked my father what made the man that way. "Well," said my Dad, "supposing we were to buy the house belonging to the Bradys (as it happens, the parents of Paul Brady the singer were our neighbours). And we moved in, only to find that Mrs Brady was still using the kitchen! We would say, politely but firmly, that this was our house now. Then suppose we found Mr Brady upstairs still working on projects, we would tell him we needed, indeed we now owned, all the rooms. Suppose we found their son in the attic at the weekend, we'd say the same. Now, you remember about inviting Jesus into your life? The difference in that man we saw this evening is that he has allowed Jesus into all the rooms in his life." Travelling together that evening between Derry and Strabane, in his little Ford Escort van, my father taught me a lot of what I know about being filled with the Holy Spirit.

Command and promise

The two key words to remember about being filled with the Spirit are 'command' and 'promise.' 'Command' because Ephesians 5:18 tells us, "Be filled." 'Promise' because "This is the confidence we have in approaching God: that if we ask anything according to his will, he hears us. And if we know that he hears us – whatever we ask – we know that we have what we asked of him."[26] I think by this time you're beginning to catch the drift that it is indeed God's will that we be filled with the Holy Spirit. So what would happen if you asked him to do that now? He will respond. His promise is your guarantee.

There's nothing magic about these words but they will help to consolidate your request to God: "Father I need you. I acknowledge trying to run my own life without you, which has been wrong. I now invite Christ to take control of my life again. Fill me with your Holy Spirit as you promised. Thank you. Amen."

If this expresses what you want to say, talk to God now and ask him to fill you with the Holy Spirit.

Decisive and progressive

It's great to have a concrete opportunity like this to be filled with the Spirit but, as we have seen, he has only begun what he wants to do in us. So there is a decisive element in being filled – like asking him just now. And there is a progressive element because he takes on more of your life as you grow to trust him with more. We'll talk about that next. Remember too that though you may feel great that's not how we know whether we are filled with the Spirit (you may even feel perfectly ordinary!). We know because of the promise of his Word.

Meanwhile expect God to use you. For starters, why not talk to someone new about Christ, see what happens and watch God work.

---

26 1 John 5:14,15

CHAPTER 4

WALKING – FRESH AND BALANCED

When the New Testament writers were looking for a word to best describe our normal progress in life they chose 'walking' as the most common way to express it (over 50 times). It is the very normality of it that is so striking. This includes 'walking' in love, in faith, in truth, in obedience, in the Spirit, worthy of our calling. Walking is putting one foot in front of the other, it is moving on, not standing still, not vegetating, not waiting to see if something happens. I am going to suggest four major factors that will help you "keep in step with the Spirit" as Paul puts it to the Galatians, "Since we live by the Spirit, let us keep in step with the Spirit."[1] These factors are:

    (a) practise spiritual breathing

    (b) know your resources as a child of God

    (c) be prepared for spiritual conflict

    (d) live by faith.

We will look at the first two now and the second two in the next chapter.

(a) Practise spiritual breathing

In chapter two we looked at 'breathing out' – confessing sin as a prerequisite to enjoying fellowship with Christ. This is not a once-and-for-all experience. When we become aware again of rebellion in our hearts towards God we have the opportunity to confess and keep going. This has often been called 'keeping short accounts with God.' Maybe we should call it proceeding on a 'cash only' basis! In chapter three we considered the great privilege all believers have in being filled with the Holy Spirit. We get nothing done without him. That's like breathing in. I'll never forget the birth of our elder son. When he drew his first breath it was a dramatic sound! It was like he had never done this before – well, he hadn't! Then he breathed out again and had another go. I watched each breath in amazement. Nowadays, of

---

[1] Galatians 5:25

course, he's a professional. He breathes all the time. And that's a good habit for us to get into in our 'spiritual breathing' too.

Not a leap in the dark

Christian faith is no 'leap in the dark.' The Bible specifically teaches that our life as believers is designed not as a leap in the dark but as a "walk in the light". Here's how John puts it: "If we walk in the light, as he is in the light, we have fellowship with one another, and the blood of Jesus, his Son, purifies us from all sin."[2] When I first encountered the power of this passage as a student I could understand the first part all right – that walking with God made for good fellowship with others. That sounds logical, doesn't it? It was the next part that I took my time over. It appeared to be saying that while I walk in the light the blood of Jesus is dealing with my sin. But this mention of sin sounded to me more like walking in the dark. Surely "walking in the light" meant being up there with the spiritual greats of all time, maybe Saint Patrick, Saint Brigid, some missionary guy in Africa we've never heard of, or my mother. But the only logical explanation turned out to be that, while I walk in the light, sin will naturally be made clear to me and I have the right to claim God's forgiveness and keep walking!

I had always subscribed to the theory (I don't know where I got it, I think I just made it up) that when you had done something displeasing to the Lord you were useless in the witness department until you had confessed and then waited a good while for life to perk up. So when I was a student in Trinity College I would set out from my rooms in the Graduates Memorial Building in the morning, to go to the lab (in the Moyne Institute across the park) where I studied, with every intention of bearing witness for Christ. I would be scarcely halfway there when Satan would sidle up to me and say, "When you think about it, you're not much of

---
[2] 1 John 1:7

an advertisement for Christianity are you? Are you really sure all your sins are forgiven? Have you put a couple of miles of clear blue water between yourself and the past?" (Satan seems to be very fussy about who gets to share their faith! He wouldn't mind if we all got neutralised by any old plausible-sounding argument.) By the time I reached the lab my resolution had been torpedoed.

Keeping it practical

So you can imagine that getting my head around "walking in the light" was, to put it mildly, a big break. I attended an evangelism training session in Greystones, County Wicklow, one Saturday morning where we studied this passage together. Then the guy running it said, "Just to keep it practical ..." and I was sure he was going to suggest that we had a time of prayer to take some deliberate steps to breathe spiritually (although we had already done that in private). But no, that wasn't his idea. "Just to keep it practical we'll get in the cars now and go to Dun Laoghaire Pier to see whom we can talk to about the Lord." "Cars!" I panicked internally, "Nobody said anything about cars! The Pier! Good grief! I might know somebody there! Anyway, I'm not ready. I'm not all prayed up. How do I know if I'm even filled with the Holy Spirit? I mean, you have to have a glowing feeling in the back of your neck before you go out boldly to talk to other people, don't you?" I was rescued by the word of God that reminded me that we "walk by faith" – and by the arrival of the cars. (Apparently we were going to drive by faith too.)

Thirty-five minutes later I found myself walking down Eblana Avenue in Dun Laoghaire where I fell into conversation with a fellow in his late teens who was sitting on the low wall at the corner with Marine Road. After talking around the subject for a while I asked him if he had any interest in knowing God personally. He did. Since I wasn't quite expecting this it took me a moment to recover and find in my jacket pocket a user-friendly outline of the gospel. I asked whether he would be up for the two of us going through this four-point outline together. "Why not?" So, between us, we read through the outline, covering half a dozen key Bible passages that spoke into his situation. Then came the time to pop the question. "Would you like to invite Christ to come into your life?" I asked. "Yes." By this point I had lost the plot since my mental script didn't run this far. I couldn't remember what I had been trained to do in these situations (not really having imagined myself getting into such situations!) So I improvised. "Here's a sample prayer you could pray. Take the booklet home and kneel down at your bedside and pray and Christ will keep his promise to come in." (I can't believe I said that – when I kneel down by my bedside I fall asleep!) Once I had packed him off home I'm sure God looked after him and I later learned, and am still learning, how to do better. I never did meet him again. But when I looked back over all that had happened in our conversation that afternoon I could see something from which I have never since recovered. God used me in someone else's life. Allowing God to fill me with his Spirit had made a difference. Just like those first disciples who were told, "You will receive power when the Holy Spirit comes on you; and you will be my witnesses."[3]

Working through the backlog

Now I wanted to see what would happen back at the lab. Life isn't all wandering around the Pier talking to strangers. Walking in the Spirit the best I knew how, I went in on Monday morning and said to the girl who worked beside me at the bench, "I know this sounds rather sheepish but we have worked side by side for a couple of years and I have never told you about the most important thing in my life – and that is a person, who is Jesus Christ." "Before you get too far," she said, "let me tell you something. I'm a Christian too. I come from a missionary family and I've never told you. Haven't we both been silly billies?!"

---
3   Acts 1:8

In the months that followed, between the lab and Dun Laoghaire Pier, I learned to practise spiritual breathing. There was a little backlog of witness to deal with at the lab, as I have mentioned, and yes, we (who had taken the training in evangelism) did go back to the Pier because it turned out that anybody who was anybody among the arty types hung out there. So we became arty types too and helped them form the "New Ireland Arts Laboratory" through which we made great friends, some of whom will be joining us in eternity. We called it NIAL and thought that was really cool. I also learned more than I had planned about copper enamelling and printing poetry.

Just like God to do it this way

An arrangement for walking in sunshine is what we might expect of God because of who he is. He isn't a frivolous Father who chuckles as he leaves us to have a go on our own. But popular (and uninformed) opinion has come to think of God as begrudging and ungenerous. A business friend with whom I was studying "walking in the light" in 1 John 1:7 said, "Wait a minute. If this passage is saying what I think it's saying then I have been taught something completely different for twenty years! I thought that the Christian life was mostly in the dark and we got to see a shaft of light only once in a while. It looks like we can continue to walk in the light and, on reflection, it's more like God to do it that way."

When we talk about walking in the Spirit and spiritual breathing we don't mean being in darkness and light on alternate days. You can "keep in step with the Spirit," trust God's cleansing for sin as and when you recognise and forsake it, and enjoy the experience of seeing God use you. That way, you can live in the light. You will, of course, step into the dark if you intentionally re-take the driving seat of your life and entertain sin instead of confessing it.

You will remember our instruction is, "Be filled with the Spirit"[4] and God's promise is that he hears us when we ask according to what he wants[5]. This promise holds good despite your circumstances. Maybe you're thinking, "But you don't know my situation." God does know your situation and is ready now to fill you with his Spirit. Perhaps you are wondering whether you need to wait until you are getting on better with your parents or your spouse. Don't wait! Doesn't it make more sense to let God work through you, to enable you, for your part, to respond well? Spiritual breathing isn't something for religious settings. Let God work in your life to meet those very same circumstances, like setbacks at work, a history of disappointment with yourself, blown relationships, or the hormones which affect us all.

Delicate relationships

A believing student told me how she had gone home for the university term break and 'lost it' with her parents. She felt embarrassed, ashamed, grubby because it looked like she had lost her reputation with them. When she returned in the new term it seemed pointless and hypocritical to set up again as a nice-girl Christian. She wondered whether walking in the Spirit was even going to be an option. But what had happened to her is not that unusual for university students and their parents, whether or not they are believers. The scenario goes like this: Parents wish student would hurry up with their Leaving Cert and leave. The day comes. Student leaves for university, mother cries. Student visits home (probably with washing) months later. Everybody gets mad. Why? Because they only know old patterns of responding to each other. Despite the fact that everybody has changed a little there hasn't been time to practise new behaviour patterns with each other. This is especially poignant when the student has decided to follow Christ and has seen that the change,

---

4   Ephesians 5:18

5   1 John 5:14,15

so far, has been for the good. Does spiritual breathing work in this situation which is, after all, a common dilemma of coming of age? Course it does.

Not only does it 'work' but I would suggest that this scenario is so important in life that anything short of spiritual breathing will be a blunt instrument with which to bring the necessary soothing. In fact if the day-by-day, moment-by-moment filling of the Holy Spirit doesn't work at home, where life is never more real, what use is it? Immediately after Paul told the Ephesians to be filled with the Spirit he helpfully listed for them the life situations where they could most expect to see the effects of Christ living in and through them. These situations – attitude of wives to their husbands, husbands to their wives, children to their parents, fathers to their children, employees' attitudes at work, and employers' attitudes – are the intricate, delicate, vital relationships in life that require nothing short of 'full power,' like it says on microwave ovens. Even when you think you're completely on your own in wanting to live a godly life in the midst of such challenges – remember there is someone else there, Christ himself, who has promised, "Never will I leave you; never will I forsake you."[6]

As you walk with Christ, breathing spiritually will always help to keep you fresh. The next factor, knowing your resources, will keep you balanced.

(b) Know your resources as a child of God

At this point, we have only started on the catalogue of resources, which has already been made available to you. A group of about a dozen new Christians used to meet in our home in Galway to study the Bible. We began with the first few verses of Ephesians which includes the words, "Praise be to the God and Father of our Lord Jesus Christ, who has blessed us in the heavenly realms

---

6 Hebrews 13:5

with every spiritual blessing in Christ."[7] This passage, like the rest of Ephesians chapter one, has such concentrated content that you can't easily gulp it all down at once. It's like eating chocolates. The section quoted looks like a compressed hymn with all the padding squeezed out. So we were all brought up short by Tom, a student from Donegal, who blurted out, "Oh no, it can't mean that!"

"What do you mean, Tom?" I said.

"Well, are you saying that God has already given us all these blessings?"

"Yep," we all said, "seems to be what the Bible says here."

"But that would be incredible," Tom persisted, "imagine us here possessing all this stuff! Just look at the shape of us!"

"That's Ephesians for you," we smugly confirmed, with an attitude that meant, "Where have you been all these years; every card-carrying believer knows this sort of thing."

"But hang on," persisted the irrepressible Tom, "every blessing?"

Only then did we begin to slow down and learn an important lesson from Tom, and from God. Could it just be that God has indeed lodged into your account every single conceivable thing that you will ever, in a hundred years, need to live life? You're loaded! Let's examine some of your inheritance. (This is exciting – it's a bit like reading a will.)

Membership

You have automatic membership in the Christian family. Romans explains this: "You received the Spirit of sonship. And by him we cry, 'Abba, Father.' The Spirit himself testifies with our spirit that we are God's children. Now if we are children, then we are heirs – heirs of God and co-heirs with Christ."[8] "Abba" was the word for 'Dad' in Jesus' home language (Aramaic) when he was on earth. And now we can address God on the same terms. He even

---

[7] Ephesians 1:3

[8] Romans 8:15-17

calls us "co-heirs with Christ." This concept is similar to land succession rights – there are different inheritance systems. Over the centuries in Ireland, for example, a farmer's land would be literally divided up between his children (which often made for decreasingly small fields). But there is another system by which two sons could jointly own and work a field — and it is this idea that is presented when we are called Christ's "co-heirs." Our association with him has automatically conferred on us the full rights of family members. This is not membership you need to apply for, like 'membership offers' you get in junk mail. This is a paid-up life membership, already made out in your name, that you can call on as soon as you like.

Family rights

Being related to Christ in this way has two massive implications. First, you belong to somebody now. For those who have waited all their life to have "someone to watch over me" – now there is someone who loves you who is constantly looking out for your welfare. Second, if you are God's child, and so am I, what does that make us? Brothers! (Or brother and sister!) Belonging to Christ is our highest and overriding identity on earth. What unites Christians is not where we come from (our backgrounds couldn't be more dissimilar) but where we are going, because of who we belong to. If there is anything I can do for you, it is a priority for me, because we are in the top family.

This membership scheme has special protection too. Paul continues, just in case you were wondering, "Who shall separate us from the love of Christ? Shall trouble or hardship or persecution or famine or nakedness or danger or sword? ... In all these things we are more than conquerors through him who loved us. For I am convinced that neither death nor life, neither angels nor demons, neither the present nor the future, nor any powers, neither height nor depth, nor anything else in all creation, will be able to separate us from the love of God that is in Christ Jesus our Lord."[9] That settles that then.

Balanced diet

If we think of the Holy Spirit as the oxygen of our life, then the Bible is the food for our soul. You can't go more than a few minutes without breathing physically but it is food that builds up your body as time goes by. In the same way our intake of the Bible provides the nourishment we need to give us strength. Note that discipline in Bible-reading, however commendable, is not the source of our life. (The Pharisees did lots of Bible study.) We live by faith and God's Spirit supernaturally switches on and empowers our spirits. But if you are ever going to grow you need to be fed and that must come from God's Word. There is simply no such thing as a growing, going-for-it Christian who is not deeply involved with the Bible. If we needed any underlining of this idea the Lord Jesus did that himself at his first big temptation. Remember what he said to Satan? "Man does not live on bread alone but on every word that comes out of the mouth of God" (Matthew 4:4). He proceeded to quote the Bible appropriately at every turn of temptation. We too are to use the Bible in the hand-to-hand combat that faces every believer. In Paul's inventory of spiritual armour the final piece is "the sword of the Spirit which is the word of God."[10]

Getting a grip

Here's a simple and effective way to illustrate what it means to 'get a grip' on the Bible. It's like getting a grip on anything else; it takes all four fingers and your thumb, in this case fingers one to four representing hearing, reading, studying and memorising and the thumb representing meditating on the word of God. Let's take them in order.

---

9 Romans 8:35,37-39

10 Ephesians 6:17

Hearing – sometimes it is good to meet with others just to hear the Bible read out loud. You always see angles in it you might not get otherwise. There are various online recordings of the Bible which can have the same effect while driving, walking, or working around the house.

Reading – maybe you're an organised person and will come up with a handy plan to read through the Bible. I'm not and so I have used other people's systems that have arranged the content of the Bible over a year or so. That way I can keep reading into new areas that I might not have chosen at random or by returning to my favourites. There are various simple reading plans like this published. Air-traffic control wouldn't work very well if the radar was only aimed at one small sector of the sky! Likewise, make sure you make use of the full scope of what God has provided for us. Another way to think of the Bible is God's lifelong conversation with us. What would it be like if your conversations with your best friend, or your spouse or your sister were always controlled by their agenda, not yours? What if it went like that for years? Of course God is always ready to listen to your agenda but you can imagine the quality that will come into your relationship when you allow him to steer the conversation with his agenda, the Bible.

Studying the Bible is not the exclusive preserve of those who are officially kitted out to do it through their specialised education. You can have a go yourself. Since the Bible was written book by book by many different authors that's a good place to start – start with a single book. Ask of it the questions you would ask of any other book, like,

- "Why was this book written?"
- "What was the main big thing the writer was saying?"
- "Why did God include this in his inspired Bible?"
- "What other part of the Bible does this remind me of?"

Once you have found your way around the Bible you might want to launch an investigation into a certain theme that runs through it.

By this time you will probably have thought of the advantages of **memorising** particular passages. In the Psalms David says, "I have hidden your word in my heart that I might not sin against you."[11] If you want to be equipped for life there is no better way than to commit significant passages of God's word to memory. These may be as short as one or two verses at a time, or a consecutive passage, like a chapter. Before you say, "My memory's useless, I could never memorise anything like that!" let me encourage you. My Spanish friends tell me that taxi drivers in Barcelona memorise an amount of geographical material similar to the length of the New Testament! Medical students commit to memory a vast amount of information just in learning anatomy. You yourself probably know a surprising string of numbers like your mobile number, usernames, passwords, a couple of PIN numbers and scores of historic football matches in their correct years. Go on, spoil yourself, start a little Bible memorisation this week. Find a friend who wants to do the same and help each other by checking what you each have learned every week, say. It will soon pay dividends in your thought-life and effectiveness. Start with something simple. The Holy Spirit will never bring back to your memory a verse that you haven't put in there in the first place.

Meditating

I mentioned that meditating is like the thumb when it comes to "gripping" Scripture – and Scripture gripping you! Meditation has come to mean, for some people, thinking about another deity or about nothing or about a nice thought. That's not what we're talking about here. In Christian life, meditating on what you have

---

11 Ps 119:11

already read and probably memorised is a vital way of making the Bible a part of your life. Like a cow chewing the cud to get all the good out of the grass, we need to take it slowly sometimes and think deeply about what we read. One simple way to do this would be to take a sentence and go over it again and again, each time emphasising a different word. Try it with an example like "Do not be anxious about anything, but in everything, by prayer and petition, with thanksgiving, present your requests to God."[12] You could start with thinking about "Do not be anxious" – it is an instruction. Then you could move on to emphasising "anxious" and think about what exactly it means. Then "Do not be anxious about anything" (that's a big statement!) and so on. Now you're getting the idea, try it on a favourite verse of your own.

Direct line

We're spoiled when it comes to another of our resources – prayer. It's hard for us to imagine what life was like for the disciples when they wanted to approach God about something. First they had to find Jesus, who could have been doing anything that particular day. They would put their question to him and he would go and talk to his Father about it – maybe in one of their all-night sessions. Jesus would come down the mountain in the morning and tell the disciples what the outcome was. As you can imagine, there were limits to doing things this way. So, as it came near the time for Jesus to go to the cross, he said to the disciples, "I will see you again and you will rejoice, and no-one will take away your joy. In that day you will no longer ask me anything. I tell you the truth, my Father will give you whatever you ask in my name. Until now you have not asked for anything in my name. Ask and you will receive, and your joy will be full."[13]

---

12 Philippians 4:6

13 John 16: 23,24

Radical idea

This was a radical idea. You could just go to God as Father directly – even if you were a bit of a nobody without religious pedigree. All you had to do was turn up and say, "Jesus sent me." You would instantly become a somebody as far as the Father was concerned. This is what we call praying 'in Jesus' name.' No more need for the old roundabout request system. The Father would gladly receive approaches from anybody who belonged to Jesus. He would delight in answering requests that he knew were along the lines of his will, long since worked out with the Son. This is what we mean by God answering our prayers 'for Jesus' sake.' This was obviously new thinking for the disciples so Jesus put it to them another way. "In that day you will ask in my name. I am not saying that I will ask the Father on your behalf. No, the Father himself loves you because you have loved me and have believed that I came from God."[14] It wasn't long before they said, "Now you are speaking clearly and without figures of speech."[15] They'd got it! How did they feel the first time they talked to God on their own? It must have been riveting stuff to see the Father answer prayer just like Jesus had in person but now, like they did in the book of Acts, you could do it anywhere! The next thing you know they are approaching God, not just from the Temple in Jerusalem, but from Cyprus, Turkey, Greece, Malta and Italy. And it worked! Because now believers, wherever they were, had the Holy Spirit living in them, enabling this new prayer privilege to be exercised anywhere, day or night.

---

14 John 16: 26,27
15 John 16:29

Diplomatic status

One of the other rights you have inherited as God's child is the position of being an ambassador. You represent his kingdom to that unique group with whom you will come into contact. This tells me something about the dignity of belonging to Christ. Ambassadors are supposed to act with poise. Not only do they know and present their country's position on just about anything, their lifestyle will also be watched closely. They are, for many people in their host country, the only available example of someone from the ambassador's home country. Not everyone in the new country will see things the ambassador's way (that's why he is sent there in the first place) but even in expressing differences he keeps his equilibrium. Criticism doesn't affect him like it would others because, after all, he reports to the person who sent him from that home country. He does all he possibly can to fit in with his host culture but it's not unusual for him to get up in the morning and think, "I belong somewhere else." However, this is a feeling that comes with the territory. It's part of being an ambassador. The Irish ambassador to India lived on our street in Dublin. We never saw much of him because, of course, to fulfil his main job he wasn't intending to be in Ireland but in India! In chapters 6 and 7 we will look at the practical implications of being a great ambassador for Christ. There is no substitute for ambassador work if you want to grow up as a Christian.

So there you have it – freshness and balance – just what you'd expect to keep your 'walking' on the go. This will mean practising spiritual breathing and getting the best out of the rights which belong to you. These rights include family membership, Bible intake, talking things over with your Father and being an ambassador. Quite a list.

CHAPTER 5

WALKING THROUGH WAR, BY FAITH

Now, there are two more vital factors if you want to make good progress. The first is a frank look at the war zone we live in. The second is living by faith. That's what gives us the edge in making headway against the odds.

(a) Be prepared for spiritual conflict

I would be unfair to you if I did not tell you that you have three enemies – the world, the flesh and the devil. I want to talk about this because it's better to know now what's in store than to have a nasty surprise that you weren't prepared for. Ephesians puts it this way, "Put on the armour of God, so that when the day of evil comes, you may be able to stand your ground, and after you have done everything, to stand."[1] Notice that we are to get ready beforehand so that we are equipped when the day comes. And notice also that when the dust settles you will still be there. Standing! I hear people talk about spiritual warfare sometimes as if this was a battle you were fated to lose. When the slightest thing goes wrong with their life they are inclined to say, "Oops, here comes spiritual warfare." But things go wrong for everybody – believers and unbelievers alike. The question that shows what you're made of is – how do you respond? We are in an unusual war because we know the final outcome. That's part of what Jesus won for us through his death. Let's take the enemies one at a time.

Private enemy No.1 – The world

The Lord told a parable about a farmer sowing seed.[2] Some of the seed didn't get on too well in growing because it fell in the wrong places. One seedling never made it because the sun scorched it when the rocky soil didn't give it enough sustenance. Another dangerous place was among thorns which choked the seedling.

---

1 Ephesians 6:13
2 Matthew 13:1-23

Jesus went on to explain that the fate of the seeds in these substandard soils represented the pressure that comes on someone who has heard God's message but gets stung with criticism from their peers (the sunburn problem) or the pressure generated by simply living in a hostile environment which uses up your brain on chasing money and worry about life (the choking problem). What to do about it?

John simply says, "Never give your hearts to the world or to any of the things in it. A man cannot love the Father and love the world at the same time. For the whole world-system, based as it is on men's primitive desires, their greedy ambitions and the glamour of all that they think splendid, is not derived from the Father at all, but from the world itself. The world and all its passionate desires will one day disappear. But the man who is following God's will is part of the permanent and cannot die."[3] We are not to "give our hearts" to the world-system around us, no matter how much 'everybody's doing it.' Where is your emotional home? Where does your heart come home to roost after a hard day's flight?

To win this particular round you will need to let your higher allegiance to Jesus kick into play. That is going to give you the advantage you need. His commentary: "In this world you will have trouble. But take heart! I have overcome the world."[4] And he is someone who knows what he is talking about since he took the trouble to come here and see and experience it for himself.

Private enemy No.2 – The flesh

You are a war zone just at present because, if you're still reading this, you are alive in the flesh. And that means you have two vested interests working on you at the same time! "The sinful nature [a rather more polite way of saying 'the flesh'] desires

---

3   1 John 2:15-17 trans J.B. Phillips

4   John 16:33

what is contrary to the Spirit, and the Spirit what is contrary to the sinful nature. They are in conflict with each other, so that you do not do what you want. But if you are led by the Spirit, you are not under Law."[5] Don't get me wrong here – I'm not saying that two equal and opposite forces are warring for your soul and nobody is sure who'll win, like in some sci-fi movie. As you will have noticed, we are not "under Law," suffering from the constant embarrassment of getting it wrong, if we are led by the Spirit.

In our bad old days we were stuck with our sinful nature – there was really nothing we could do about it. That's the difference. Now, although we won't get rid of the sinful nature till we go to heaven we are not obliged to do its bidding. Paul goes on to tell the Romans, "We have an obligation – but it is not to the sinful nature, to live according to it. For if you live according to the sinful nature, you will die; but if by the Spirit you put to death the misdeeds of the body, you will live."[6] In other words, you can no longer say, "The devil made me do it." You have a choice now and not even the devil can stand against you when you choose to be led by the Spirit.

Making the music

During the Cold War it was not unusual for one side or the other to provide free radios for a rural countryside in a nation whose hearts and minds they were trying to take over. The only odd thing about the radios was that they had no tuning knob to choose the wavelength. There was a control for volume and an on-off switch but no tuning – because that had been decided for you! It only received one frequency and, as you can imagine, that brought the message from your 'benefactor.' Of course they threw in a bit of music too. But you were obliged to listen to one station.

---

5 Galatians 5:17,18

6 Romans 8:12,13

If, on the other hand, you came into our kitchen today you would expect to find a radio with a tuning dial, and you'd be right. I can choose whether I listen to Lyric FM, Radio Nova, 2fm, Q102 or whatever. But would you congratulate me on making the music? Would you say, "That's a wonderful example of Beethoven, (or classic rock or mood music or Gregorian chant). How do you do it?" Such a comment wouldn't make any sense. All I have to do is turn the dial, scarcely worthy of congratulation, and out comes the music. It is produced by somebody else, somewhere else. Similarly if you get up tomorrow morning and say, "Lord Jesus, here I am. I'm hopeless at running my own life and I want you to take control throughout today. I hereby choose the frequency, please produce the music," then he will give you the power to "put to death the misdeeds of the body" as you go through the day trusting him to deliver the goods.

Why do aeroplanes fly?

The sinful nature has not disappeared but a greater force can keep it under control. An Aer Lingus pilot friend explains it this way. A 747 on the runway can weigh about 300 tonnes. No way is this amount of bulk metal going anywhere. But once you have it tanked up, taken it to the end of a runway and trundled it along the ground approaching a couple of hundred miles an hour, it proceeds to do that very thing your mind says it should not do. Three hundred tonnes of metal flies though the air. Why? Has the plane got lighter? Has the law of gravity evaporated? No, but other laws, laws of aerodynamics, have proved stronger.

I hope you haven't skipped this bit for any reason. The flesh is an enemy so close you can make the mistake of forgetting about it. After all, everybody has heard about the devil and the world but the "sinful nature" – what's that? The sexual nuances in the office that are passed off as 'a bit of a laugh' can become the gun you didn't know was loaded.

Private enemy No.3 – The devil

The author of *The Chronicles of Narnia,* C.S. Lewis, wisely commented that Satan has two basic strategies. One is to have people forget about him so that he can get on with his work. The other is to have everybody concentrate on him, thus robbing God of worship.[7] Our culture at present has a certain fascination with horror, evil and vampires. Despite the fact that crime is to be found in any Western society how can every week's TV schedules need so much programming about 'serial killers'? Satan, however, is a master of deception and his image in the popular mind has more to do with cartoons (showing Satan with a pitchfork) than with his reality as exposed in the Bible. This false image can easily get implanted in your mind if you're not careful, so let's look at what we can be sure of.

Yes, the devil is an enemy of our souls but he is not invincible. Peter tells us that he is like "a roaring lion looking for someone to devour." In the next breath he goes on to say, "Resist him, standing firm in the faith"[8] to which James adds, "Resist the devil, and he will flee from you. Come near to God and he will come near to you."[9] Again Paul says, "Put on the full armour of God so that you can take your stand against the devil's schemes."[10] Not only is Satan's power limited and his fate sealed by Christ's death on the cross, but his schemes here on earth are known and finite and God has given us countermeasures.

Countermeasures

Amongst the devil's favourite but less well-known strategies is encouraging people not to forgive one another. So Paul tells his friends in Corinth about someone he had forgiven: "I have

---

7 C.S. Lewis *The Screwtape Letters* (Grand Rapids: Zondervan, 2001), ix

8 1 Peter 5:9

9 James 4:7,8

10 Ephesians 6:11

forgiven in the sight of Christ for your sake, in order that Satan might not outwit us. For we are not unaware of his schemes."[11] I got a letter some while ago from someone saying they had forgiven me for a wrong for which I had asked forgiveness. It is a happy occasion when somebody does this – because the granting of forgiveness is rare. It is rare, it is Christian and it is a primary countermeasure against the devil. He does not have forgiveness in his armoury. So when someone asks you for forgiveness this is not a time to say, "It's OK," "Forget it," "No probs," "We all have our failings." Learn how to say, "I forgive you." Remember, forgiving can stop Satan "outwitting us."

Why does it work when we "resist the devil"? It works because "the one who is in you is greater than the one who is in the world".[12] We need to know our enemy but we have nothing to fear from him. Christ became as human as we are "so that by his death he might destroy him who holds the power of death – that is, the devil – and free those who all their lives were held in slavery by their fear of death."[13]

Our enemy will sometimes go all out to tempt us but remember that experiencing temptation is not sin. We sin when we give in to temptation and make provision for it. Often you will feel like you are the only person on earth to face this particular dilemma. But be encouraged – "No temptation has seized you except what is common to man. And God is faithful; he will not let you be tempted beyond what you can bear. But when you are tempted, he will also provide a way out so that you can stand up under it."[14] I think that's pretty good but Christ himself has gone one better. You can't beat this – "We have one who has been tempted in every way, just as we are – yet without sin. Let us then approach

---

11 2 Corinthians 2:10-11

12 1 John 4:4

13 Hebrews 2:14,15

14 1 Corinthians 10:13

the throne of grace with confidence."[15] More than once I have looked up into the sky and said, "Lord, you were once attacked with temptation just like I am feeling now. It's time to get me outta here."

(b) Live by faith

Don't let anybody fool you into thinking that life is going to be a doddle for you just because you have become a Christian. An adventure? – yes; a doddle? – no. We start as we mean to go on, and that's by faith. Faith is not hoping against hope that something nice will happen about which God has said nothing at all. We put our daily faith, not just faith for salvation, in God himself and what he has committed himself to in black and white. Neither do we have faith 'in faith.' That's like trying to moor a boat by swinging the anchor around your head and dropping it in the boat again. When Paul quotes "the righteous shall live by faith"[16] he's saying that's the only way they are going to make it – by faith. That's how they live their daily lives – they only got their righteousness by faith anyway. This is a good thing to remember when you are helping others. You don't want them to learn dependence on you as the time goes by. They need to learn to trust God more – that's what growing up spiritually consists of. Let them see how you trust God. Do you ever pray and ask for God's help and guidance when they are there with you? That might be a good idea because you don't want to give the impression that you do all this in your own strength.

The New Testament assures us that there are times when living by faith is the only thing that will pull us through because we simply cannot see what's going to happen next: "We live by faith, not by sight."[17] More often than not it is our actions that show our faith. The Bible's massive chapter on faith (Hebrews

---

15 Hebrews 4:15,16

16 Romans 1:17

17 2 Corinthians 5:7

chapter 11) is like all the quintessential action movies rolled into one screenplay. Why? Because taking risks based on what God has said is what faith is. You never saw so many risks in one place as in Hebrews 11. What classy people! Which is not to say that they all came out of their experiences with the Nobel prize. Some got it in the neck (literally) through persecution – the text says that the world wasn't worthy of them![18] But in the end they had the satisfaction of knowing that their daring had been well founded because "without faith it is impossible to please God" (verse 6).

One way to demonstrate faith is by being thankful – "Give thanks in all circumstances, for this is God's will for you in Christ Jesus."[19] Many of us want to know what God's will is for us. Well, here's a good place to start! You will notice that he specifies "all" circumstances. When I give thanks while the going is rough, this says to God, "I believe you are bigger than the difficulties I can see in front of me." Maybe you are facing an insurmountable situation in which it is difficult to thank God. Let me ask you – do you still believe that God loves you? Do you believe that he has a loving plan for your life? Do you believe that he is bigger than your present circumstances? Giving thanks to him is a profound way of communicating, "I believe. I believe you do love me and care for me." Sometimes it's the little things in life that grate on us and take away our joy. Be ready to thank God about them too.

A good reason we can afford to thank God is because Romans tells us that, "In all things God works for the good of those who love him, who have been called according to his purpose."[20] He is not saying, "Oh don't worry your little head – I bet you things will come out OK in the end." He is very specific. God is thinking about us and he has a way of re-cycling the circumstances that

---

[18] Hebrews 11:38

[19] 1 Thessalonians 5:18

[20] Romans 8:28

distress us, the forces that buffet us, the pains that wound us *and* our own mistakes. Don't you find that amazing? Notice that God's re-working is "for the good of those who love him." This is not the hard-life philosophy that says, "You win some, you lose some; get used to it." He is taking all the elements of your life (imagine!) and weaving them together for your good. He never forgets you were "called according to his purpose" and his purpose is to turn you into a masterpiece. In the midst of a stormy life this is a whole lot better than being vaguely told to keep your chin up – you could get that kind of banal generality down the pub.

The suggestions in these two chapters will keep you on an even keel and keep you going. Don't say I didn't tell you about the battles you will face. But you can win, in Christ's strength, and keep walking.

CHAPTER 6

RECOMMENDATION

When it comes to recommending Christ to others beyond our home environment, where do you think would be a natural place to start? Surely it is with the people with whom we spend the most time – like at work.

On the job

My first job was in the microbiology research department at University College Galway (later NUI Galway). We were dedicated to the manipulation of all kinds of microbes. I was working on blue-green algae to see if we could prevent them clogging up the navigation of the world's rivers and get them to maybe grow in the sea instead to provide protein food for the future (as you may have noticed, it hasn't worked, so far!). Others in the department worked on a wide range of similar issues – one of them was trying to get the best biological work out of lightning when it hits the ground and there are particular plants around. Although each of us had an independent project to pursue we were packed in the room like sardines, sharing quite a lot of the same equipment (queuing up for it, even!) drinking our morning coffee together and eating our lunch-time sandwiches, trying not to get them mixed up with the microbes.

I was well pleased to get this job. It gave me an opportunity to work at something I liked, to be supervised by a good researcher and to live in a part of the country where I wanted to be. And seeing your first pay cheque (or salary account transfer) makes you feel like an adult in a new way. One thing I didn't mention at interview was my faith in Christ. It wasn't one of the questions. I didn't mention it once the work began either. I'll bide my time, I told myself; I want to get on with these people, build friendships, show the quality of my life and integrity in my work and then the day will come when I can ask them, "Bet you're wondering why I'm such a nice guy?" That day never came. But one morning did arrive months later, at coffee time, when Jimmy, the life and soul of the office said, "We've been talking about you. You're different. We have no idea why and we intend to find out. We have therefore decided to invite ourselves over to your flat on Tuesday for a bit of a social evening so all can be revealed!" You might think I'd be pleased but part of me was mortified. How come they couldn't identify my different-ness as having something to do with following Jesus? One simple reason: I hadn't told them. They had no basic information to go on. Now I was scrambling to catch up with them, trying to explain on the one hand why Christ meant so much to me and on the other hand why it had taken me so long to get around to saying so. I can happily report that they were very generous and we got it straightened out. But right there on that evening I determined that the start of my next job was going to be different. Proverbs says, "Fear of man will prove to be a snare"[1] and I had been well and truly caught in one.

Try again

After teaching part-time for a while I went for an interview for that next job, which was to teach science at the Holy Rosary College in Mountbellew, County Galway. This time I found a way to get my faith into the interview and indeed I couldn't even offer to start on the day they wanted because I had an outstanding arrangement to help with a training conference in faith-sharing. I got the job and was introduced to that great vortex of the education system – the staff room. There I met 13 other staff and, remembering the microbe research staff horror, I took the occasions, as they presented themselves, to let my new friends know that I followed Christ, over the subsequent weeks. It was done in a low-key way, but if they saw any integrity in my work and quality in my life during my time in that school they now knew what to connect it to. Getting it clear at the beginning meant we could all relax. Opportunities for individual chats

---
1 Proverbs 29:25

began to arise, sometimes initiated by them, sometimes by me, until each one had the chance to put together the pieces of the gospel story (we're talking about many months here). At the head teacher's encouragement I went on to talk with students about personal faith in Christ. The response of the teachers, students and the head teacher varied widely but they all got to understand the basics of coming to know God in a personal way. In the end it proved to be some of the students who chose to keep faith with Christ when they went on to UCG where their faith was tested and proved true. I always knew when a former Mountbellew student greeted me in Galway – they were the only people who called me "Mr. Wilson"!

Overall occupation

Between the first job and the second I was learning to recognise that my overall occupation was recommending Christ to others. One of the first century's most enthusiastic advocates for Jesus learned this same lesson soon after they first met. Peter, by trade a fisherman, had first heard about Jesus from his brother.[2] They met, Peter was impressed and decided to follow Jesus. Peter was a lot more impressed when some time later they were out in the boat together and Jesus gave him unusual advice (which he didn't really want) about how to fish. When he reluctantly took that advice the catch was such that the one boat they had planned to put it in wasn't big enough and they had to put half the catch in a partner's boat. Not even the second boat could hold the capacity of fish and both boats began to sink. At this point Jesus had captured Peter's complete attention. Peter "fell at Jesus' knees and said, 'Go away from me, Lord; I am a sinful man.' "[3] The Lord did no such thing, but calmed Peter down and then chose that high-tension moment to tell Peter about his life's

---

2 John 1:41

3 Luke 5:4-11

overall occupation – fishing, for men. Not something Peter was likely to forget. He did another spot of fishing for fish (after the resurrection in John's Gospel account) but the big picture of what his life was about was now clear. "Follow me," Jesus said to Peter and company (and to us) "and I will make you fishers of men."[4] Our responsibility is simply to follow Jesus. His is to make us fishers of men. And if I'm never involved in fishing for men it's hard to see how I'm involved in following.

Proactively representing Jesus to others is a vital factor in your maturing. I hear people say, "Let me get a bit of maturity under my belt and then surely I'll be an effective witness." Curiously, it is the opposite that is true. Living out your role as a witness about Christ helps you mature. Not everyone is called to be an evangelist – in fact only a few are. But we all have the privilege of being witnesses and making disciples. If nothing else, it's worth it for the satisfaction of sheer obedience to Christ in this matter. And the dialogue with other people is a vast learning experience. You learn how they think. I learn more from local students who are searching for life's meaning than I do from many books that set out to prove the faith. Their very questions cause the message of Christ to shine, as different facets of the gospel meet the needs of different people.

You learn not to assume things about other people. A few months ago I was talking with a student at University College Dublin and asked him what he thought about the identity of Jesus. What I hadn't realised was that he was one of the approximately 10% students who are God-fearers but normally have no-one to talk to about spiritual matters. So he said, with some exasperation, "Exactly what it says on the tin" and when asked if he would want to know God personally said, "You'd be an idiot not to."[5]

It's a great honour to be a personal representative of Jesus of Nazareth – and to some people of your acquaintance you may

---

4 Matthew 4:19

5 *Vox* magazine (Dublin: July 2012), 33

be his only representative. And what a thrill to touch the life of another with the potential to see that life change its direction for ever. What's the greatest thing that ever happened to you? Wouldn't you say coming to know Christ? What's the greatest thing you could ever do for another? Wouldn't you say helping them to come to know him also? A letter that my wife and I keep in the front of our filing cabinet is from a young woman whose whole family, when we got to know them, were all DJs (and yes, their house had mind-boggling sound arrangements). The letter says, "I am grateful that through you I had the opportunity to hear the gospel and accept Jesus as my Lord and Saviour. Many, many thanks. As the Lord has used your lives I hope he uses mine." And the Lord is using her to alert many others to join in the grand exploit of knowing and serving him.

Have you decided what your life's overall occupation is? Are you ready to jump in and trust God in your relationships with those around you? Would you like to see heaven break loose in some of those lives you touch? If it has come to the point of wondering not *whether* you want to be a key player in their lives but *how*, then this chapter and the next are just for you. Here's how:

Be sure you are a child of God

In good training courses on how to recommend Christ to others it has proved to be helpful if we act out role-plays – such as what it is like to sit side by side with someone and give them the necessary pointers to make their own commitment to Christ. I was helping out on one of these occasions in Lucan, County Dublin, playing the part of the helpful believer with a student who had come for the training, playing the part of the happy but cooperative pagan. She played the part to perfection as I showed what the issues were, gave the options and let her 'decide.' After the mini-play was over I asked her, "When did you come to trust

Christ, in real life?" "Just now," she said. I thought she hadn't understood me but then she explained that right there in the middle of saying her lines in the script she had understood for the first time what it means to accept Christ! She was grinning from ear to ear. What a way to start – in public!

It's not that unusual for someone who is still unsure of their own position to begin thinking about telling others because they imagine this might influence God positively. (That's a waste of time – he's already as positive about you as it gets.) Maybe you think that to lead someone else to Christ would prove beyond all doubt that he is already in your life. Not so. Remember, Christ's promise is our security on this issue. If this is something you still feel wobbly about why not go back to the end of chapter one and invite him to come into your life for good.

Be sure there is no unconfessed sin in your life

In chapter two we looked at how to deal with sin that crops up in our Christian life. This can ruin our fellowship with God for a time although our relationship with him is forever secure. My wife and I dearly love our two sons and nothing will ever change that. They can't un-become our sons. Similarly your status as a child of God is not in question. But on a day to day basis you might not be experiencing friendship with him because something has got in the way. His answer: "If anybody does sin, we have one who speaks to the Father in our defence – Jesus Christ, the Righteous One. He is the atoning sacrifice for our sins."[6] Hang on to this promise and stride out in the sunshine of God's light on your path. You have the relationship with him already. Why waste time, opportunities and energy by missing out on the best fellowship with him too? When Paul was having the hardest time he burst out and wrote to his friends in Philippi, "One thing I do: forgetting what is behind and straining towards what is ahead,

---

6   1 John 2:1,2

I press on towards the goal to win the prize for which God has called me heavenwards in Christ Jesus."[7] Anything in your past that's tugging at your memory and dragging you down? Once you have confessed it to God (and others if necessary) and thanked God for his forgiveness – leave it! Maybe other people can't forget it? Not your problem now. Refer them to the Father.

Be sure you are filled with the Holy Spirit

I'm not making this up – it's exactly what Jesus told the disciples himself. To get them ready for those twilight days between his leaving and the coming of the Spirit, Jesus said to them, "You are witnesses of these things. I am going to send you what my Father has promised; but stay in the city until you have been clothed with power from on high."[8] They were witnesses already. To be a witness in court, all you have to do is see a traffic accident for example. Once you've seen it that's that – you're a witness. But Jesus knew they would be loose cannons if he gave them free range at this stage. For effectiveness they needed to be filled and powered by the Holy Spirit. After all, that was a principle reason why the Spirit was coming – to help the whole world come to understand about Jesus. The disciples and the Holy Spirit were about to go into the same line of business.

If we are going to make spiritual progress, rather than just noise, in bearing witness about Christ, we too need to be filled with his Spirit. His filling is not like a single vaccination but a day-by-day, moment-by-moment process. Maybe I learned this best from a friend at University College Galway. He and I would often meet and spend time meeting new students and sharing our faith with them. On one occasion my friend told one of these students that he'd had a hard morning, which had been spent on mending strained relationships. He further said that he

---

7 Philippians 3:13

8 Luke 24:48,49

thought the strain had been his own fault and gave some details. In my mind I was muttering to him, under my breath and through clenched teeth, "You're letting the side down man, get on with the good news," but he was in free flow by this time. Before he got around to explaining the gospel he made a throwaway remark which cast the whole conversation into a different light. He said that he was eternally grateful for God's ongoing forgiveness: "If it weren't for the Holy Spirit I don't know what I would do." At a stroke he communicated that Christians are forgiven rather than perfect, that we can't live life at all without God's implanted power, which is grounded in daily reality.

Be prepared

Sometimes those who understand about the Spirit-filled life don't feel adequate to the task of sharing their faith because they don't feel equipped. They think of this as one of life's great imponderables, a hill they will never quite climb. But take courage, it doesn't need to be that way. There are simple things you can do to prepare. "Always be prepared to give an answer to everyone who asks you to give a reason for the hope that you have," says Peter, "But do this with gentleness and respect."[9] Somehow Peter's friends had let it be known at their places of work that they had a special hope. The word was out. When it came down to answering about the details, they were to be prepared, not confrontational. Indeed, they were to be so well prepared that it was instinctive to be respectful – respectful and gentle to the *unbelievers*.

---

9   1 Peter 3:15

Straight story

Getting your story straight would be a good place to start. People love people – and stories about people. That's what sells so many magazines in supermarkets. We'll think through a number of questions that would help a colleague or acquaintance understand what is going on in your life. It is worth taking notes of your answers (just one or two sentences each).

What was your attitude before you took Christ seriously?

Remember we're talking here about the flow of normal conversation, so you don't have time to tell all about how you were actually born in Cork and what happened since. A little real-life is helpful but tell us about your attitude to other people, to yourself, to God. That's what people can identify with. It will be best to leave them wanting more. For example, if you say, "Back at that time I felt..." this implies that something different has gone on in the meantime.

Why did you begin to take Christ seriously?

Maybe it was some issue that bugged you, a family crisis, a reversal of fortunes, a big success, having a baby. I don't know, but you know and you know why this edged you further in coming to Christ. That's what's attractive – you can tell us something that nobody else knows.

How did you say "Yes" to Christ?

This time be as specific as you can in a way that would help the other person make a similar commitment. They will not have the same life circumstances as you do but they will be able to latch on to how to receive Christ if you can avoid fuzziness at this point.

What difference does following Christ make in your life?

Think. Be realistic. Now is not the time to go over the top with a phoney sales pitch. Explain simply what changes you and others have seen in your life – at the daily level and maybe at the level of your longer-term outlook. Your ability to disclose your thoughts and feelings here is a powerful, enchanting, walking advertisement for Christ.

Easy on the ear

Now, if you have taken notes, and I hope you have, look at your list of answers. Are they expressed in the sort of vocabulary that people use on the bus, in the canteen, on holiday? They need to be in 'newspaper' language because we don't want to give ourselves the extra work of teaching religious terminology do we?! Read your answers out loud. Do they sound cheesy? Or long-winded? Is the wording too specialised? Revise your answers. Be hard on yourself so you can be easy on the ear of others. Now try your answers on somebody else – maybe a friend who is not yet a believer could be more helpful. Once you are happy with what you have written, learn each sound-bite so that when the opportunity pops up you'll be ready! I use the word "pop" advisedly because that's how it happens. Issues simply come up in conversation – almost never in the order I gave above and often in various guises.

Question time

If you are waiting for people to ask you questions all the time you might have a long wait. Remember that many people sincerely mean it when they say, "Religion is an intensely personal matter" so, although they may be bursting to ask you about your faith, they are actually protecting your privacy by skirting around the issue. What breaks the spell is for you to have questions prepared too. You can use low-key, open questions like, "Where would you say you are on your spiritual journey?" This credits them with having a 'spiritual journey' but doesn't presume too much about how far it's got. During the writing of this chapter I asked this question of someone to whom I had just been introduced and it launched him into a heartfelt explanation of his struggle to find God. His response helped us find our way to the level where we could sincerely discuss how to be sure about a relationship with God. Another set of questions you may not have thought of are your own questions – "When you see all the suffering in the world on the telly – makes you think, doesn't it?" Again, I think you'll be surprised to see the fountain of interest opened up by your self-disclosure.

Knowing God personally

At some point you will need to get a grasp of the essentials of what a person needs to know to make an intelligent commitment to Christ. In Romans Paul refers to the "form" (or mould) of teaching which had brought those friends to faith.[10] They had had the basics, enough to bring them into the kingdom (now he was giving them a fuller picture). Without becoming mechanical about it you, too, need to get a mould, a basic outline of coming to know Christ. You will be a lot less mechanical once you have fixed the outline in your mind because then you can concentrate on the person in front of you rather than having to feverishly remember what should come next! I have used *Knowing God Personally* (written originally by Bill Bright, the founder of Campus Crusade for Christ/Agapé) to good effect. There are numerous other good outlines that get the main bits in and leave extraneous bits out.

Lend people good books or articles that will help to provoke

---

10 Romans 6:17

their thinking. When you refer people to an online version make sure you ask for their feedback. I suggest that you usually lend books rather than give them because it's like flying a kite – you let the string out, out, out. Then you wind it in again. Lend out a book and when it comes back be ready to ask, "What did you think of the book (or article or whatever)?", "Did it make sense to you?", "Could you identify with knowing God in the way the book talked about?" and "Would it be helpful if I explained what would be involved in taking that step?" Some will be ready for your help to come to know Christ. Lead them gently through that process. Take your time. Then make an arrangement to talk again soon to help them get going in their new life.

Some won't be ready yet to say "Yes" to Christ. Make sure you still have something else to say the next time. Introduce them to a mutual acquaintance who is a believer. Lend them a different book. Ask them what obstacles they are thinking about. You're not in a hurry. Just as fruit like raspberries ripen on different days on the same raspberry cane, people ripen at their own speed.

Landing the plane

Being able to talk about spiritual issues with a colleague may be exciting to you – but don't get so excited that you forget how normal people end a conversation, no matter how weighty. They say things like, "Are you watching the match on Saturday?" or, "I couldn't get tickets" or, "I'm not going to be in tomorrow – doing interviews, remember?" or, "When is this school ever going to get proper broadband?" In other words, they land the plane. It comes as natural as talking. And if you don't want to be known as the religious nutter around the office I suggest you "land the plane" too. This means that the next time you see that person you can say, "Why don't you support a decent team? – that was a disaster on Saturday" and they won't be on edge every time you round the corner in case you flip uninvited into religious-speak, especially when other people may be around.

Training makes the difference

Give yourself a break – take some training in how to share your faith. Even a few hours of training will help to demystify the whole process as you master a clear outline, sort out your own story and line up some good questions. A friend who had taken such training wrote from South Lebanon, where he had been serving as a major with the United Nations forces, to tell us how he had been getting on. The weekend the battalion arrived they experienced their first shelling, as a by-product of artillery exchange between the Israeli defence forces and Hezbollah. One of his colleagues turned and asked my friend if he had a "thought for the day." Quick as a flash, right off the top of his head (this is where the training comes in) he said "I do!" and shared with the three other majors present his reading from the Bible of that morning, from Psalm 91. This led to a tour of duty where officers trusted him to pass on to them what 'made him tick' and they will look back on Lebanon as the place where they heard God's word clearly. Because someone got prepared.

Pray

Before you talk to people about God it is essential to talk to God about people. This might be the most important thing you do anyway. I must confess that I am not a good pray-er and so I use the help of a notebook in which I record the names of those I want to pray for. I have made a diary section where I pray for the business of the day and the individuals I pray for every day. Then each day of the week also has three sections so I can follow in prayer (a) those who do not yet know Christ (b) those who do and are growing in him and (c) those who have taken special measures to use their lives to spread the gospel. Obviously there are many ways to accomplish the same effect – this is just my way. You need a system you are comfortable with.

But writing down your prayers and the answers will greatly

strengthen your faith. It's like watching God at work. It is watching God at work! For me it is great to see people transfer from the category (a) to the next one when they come to know Christ, and then from (b) to (c). I have watched God work in the lives of one or two who have gone through all the categories and then gone on to heaven!

Five in focus

Whatever your system is, make a list of the top five whose turning to Christ you want to pray for. As you focus on them in prayer you are already beginning to look after them. Some of them may not have anyone else to mention their name before God. You will be surprised at the opportunities that arise for you to show and explain the Christian life to those on your "five in focus" list. You are in good company to pray in such an organised way. Paul wrote to people that he was praying for them – to individuals (like Timothy and Philemon) and communities of new Christians (like at Ephesus, Colossae and Thessaloniki) including some he had never even met (like the Romans), and some whose names he seemed to know by heart: "I thank God every time I remember you. In all my prayers for all of you, I always pray with joy."[11]

There are lots of things to pray for beyond "God bless Jim." For example, you could ask God to bring Jim into contact with others who follow Jesus. You could pray that Jim gets serious in his thinking about the big issues of life, that his thoughts turn to God when life deals him a rotten hand, that God will work through other family members, that Jim will read something that stirs his spiritual interest. Stay within God's will and be inventive.

Once you're ready, you're trained and you're praying – then what? To borrow a word from Jesus, "Go!" That's where the next chapter will help us.

---

11 Philippians 1:3,4

CHAPTER 7

TAKING THE INITIATIVE

When I look at the words Jesus chose just before his ascension to heaven there is one unavoidable theme running through: "Go and make disciples of all nations"[1]; "Go into all the world and preach the good news to all creation"[2]; "I chose you and appointed you to go and bear fruit."[3] It feels like he is gently asking, "Which part of 'go' don't you understand?" Christ worded his commission to apply, not just to those disciples then, but to the succeeding generations, including you and me. We have a tendency to think, "I'm sure there are people who take care of that aspect – like missionaries, wherever they come from, right?" Wrong. We're it. Christ knows the world through and through. He knows there is no other way that the gospel will accidentally 'leak out' if we don't go. He knows how lost people are without him – in this life and the next. His conclusion? "Go."

Breaking ranks

'Going' means taking the initiative – like God did when he broke ranks and sent Jesus to get us out of trouble. For many of us 'taking the initiative' will need to include putting time for people into our schedule, maybe loosening up the schedule a bit to have time to chill and chat. Develop your own smorgasbord of chat-starters – like asking those you have talked to if you can pray for them, being vulnerable enough to ask for their help, and taking the trouble to find out what really motivates them. A sporty medical friend of ours started out a little on the reclusive side. Long-distance running was his passion – indeed cross-country was a speciality in Galway. Nobody but nobody was ever going to reach him – unless they could run alongside him. And that's exactly what happened – a lean and mean Christian, who was prepared to chat as they ran, came to run at his club. In the end he made his commitment to Christ on the track. (How can people run and talk at the same time? Beats me.)

---

1 Matthew 28:19

2 Mark 16:15

3 John 15:16

James came to faith in Christ by a completely different route. Six weeks before he came to university he saw a passage from Ephesians: "It is by grace you have been saved not by works,"[4] on a sign fixed to the wall of Merrion Hall in Lower Merrion Street in Dublin (now the Davenport Hotel). He was just passing by on the top deck of a bus! This was the missing jigsaw piece he needed. The picture fell into shape and he put his trust implicitly in Christ. He also thought he was the only person in the country to have made this discovery. I bumped into him on his first day at university and, after we introduced ourselves and talked about his course, I asked him if he knew God in a personal way. He thought, "This is happening to me again!" He told me the story of the poster and he was as amazed as I was to find that he was a brand new believer poised for take-off with no other Christian connections in the wide world. We quickly rectified that as he took on board, all in one day, assurance of his salvation, an introduction to the Bible and a noisy but loving bunch of new believing friends. He is now a responsible leader of a Christian community whose counsel is sought and appreciated by many. It didn't take much initiative to meet James but it was certainly worth it.

Talk about Jesus

You can talk about other interesting things till the cows come home but unless you talk about Jesus you're not going to be of much ultimate help. "There is no other name under heaven given to men by which we must be saved," said Peter to the Jewish leaders.[5] So we need to get around to talking about Jesus. I want to mention three obstacles to 'getting around' to talking about the useful things because if you know where the obstacles are it is easier for you to negotiate the terrain. Some people get

---

4   Ephesians 2:8-9

5   Acts 4:12

nervous as they approach each of these three points, rather like a supersonic aircraft which shudders when it passes through the speed of sound. Once you have flown through a sonic boom you return to smooth flying again.

The three sonic booms you need to be aware of are: (a) talking to people at all (b) moving from talking about general religious ideas to talk about Jesus and (c) popping the question, "Do you think you would be ready to invite Jesus into your life?" Practising how you go through these three booms will make your life easier, your conversation more natural and save you a lot of sweat.

Talking at all

As a nation we're famous for talking. But some of us squirm a bit at that reputation. If you're like me you're not much of a conversationalist. We don't all 'walk right up to people' and begin talking. So all kinds of invisible, informal conventions have arisen which license us to talk to those we may not know well, or at all. That's what the weather's *for*, after all. It is worth practising these little introductions if you're not naturally good at it. Last month I even saw a book called *How to Talk to Anyone* (by Leil Lowndes) in the Pearse Station coffee shop. If people can learn to meet others for business, or practise chat-up lines for romance, maybe I can learn to make myself accessible to those in my surroundings.

From religion to Jesus

They used to say that the taboo subjects were religion and politics. Not any longer. People can talk, on their own terms, about 'religion' and will wax eloquent about matters 'spiritual.' This is no bad thing. It gets you started. But since Jesus isn't about religion you are going to have to steer the subject, or restart it. I met up with one guy, off and on, over about three years. He was always cordial, we had good talks, but he was not yet ready to accept Christ. The next time we met he thought he would nip the subject in the bud by saying, "Of course I have no time for organised religion." "Jesus would certainly agree with you there," I said, "He seemed to be against organised religion more than most things." Off we went again, talking about Jesus this time, not religion.

At a university art gallery I met a girl who was studying world religions in her spare time. She told me about the various founders of world religions she had studied and I couldn't help noticing that she was a bit careful in how she talked because she perceived me to be a partisan Christian religionist. I made the innocent remark that I was a follower of Jesus of Nazareth rather than a religious party line. I couldn't have anticipated her response, "Exactly!" she said, almost shouting, "Exactly – it's not about religion is it? I was brought up in a very strict church background and they were against everything and it was all rules and I left." "And then?" I asked. I think she had expected me to do a walk-out protest and was surprised when I stayed! Now she talked like a shot out of a gun. "I have backed off all this religion stuff to investigate each great leader and see who's right." (This is a summary – it took her an hour to say it!) I told her she was on the right track if she remembered to include Jesus since he is unique in that he validated his claims by rising from the dead. She would have talked all day because she had found somebody ready to talk about Jesus, not religion.

Popping the question

This delicate area deserves our best attention. Nobody wants to be rushed into the kingdom of God with unseemly haste. That would be counterproductive anyway since this is a decision you want to be sure about. But many people appreciate the offer of help to make the options clear and open up the opportunity to take a definite step. A friend of mine asks those she has talked to a few times already, "Well, ready to trust Jesus yet, or are you still thinking about it?" That gently gives the option of saying "still thinking" and opens up the discussion to what the stumbling blocks might be. Of course you can simply ask, "Is there any reason why you wouldn't want to invite Christ into your life now?" or, "Can I help you with any questions that are still outstanding?" When I asked one guy what was missing – did he need more information, or more time or what? – his answer (which quite surprised me) told us what we needed to know: "I need more courage."

You haven't really communicated the gospel message completely until the question has been popped. Inherent in the gospel is this edge of challenge. It isn't a call to new intellectual rigour, it is a call to change direction and so, at some stage, the point needs to be put, "Are you ready to jump?" Many have to face this question alone but it can be a tremendous help to have someone to talk it through with. I heard a phlegmatic Ulster farmer tell how he came to this dilemma – he desperately wanted to come to God but he knew no words, none at all, to use in stepping over the line into God's kingdom. So he went out into the field and drew a line on the ground with a stick and mumbled in his mind to God, "When I step over this line that's me in." And then he stepped over the line. But not everyone needs to be that lonely!

Just between ourselves

Now can I ask about something confidential? It might just be that you have wondered if recommending Jesus to others would blow the hard-won relationships you already have. Let me ask – really, would it blow relationships? Don't you think that soul-talk pays someone a compliment, you're taking them seriously, you're treating them as a whole live person? You don't want to have fake friendships, do you? I need to say also that yes, you can lose friends who are finally uncomfortable about Jesus. You can also make friends for life and eternity by being faithful and straight with them now. And your side of the friendship will be put to the test when someone doesn't want to follow Jesus yet.

My wife grew up in a good home which was not, however, Christian in the sense of any acknowledgement of Christ. She knew nothing at all about how to know God. At 14 she went to hear the evangelist Billy Graham speak, which moved her and attracted her to the truth but she didn't understand much of what was going on. A couple of years later Janie, a friend from school, invited her to join her at a ski weekend. They skied to their heart's content and she also heard how someone could come to belong to Christ, which she promptly decided to do. Someone was on hand to help her make that step and she began her journey with Christ there in the mountains. Now, did Janie take a risk with their friendship by this invitation? I suppose she did – and I am very glad she did too! What happened to their friendship next? Who is one of my wife's best friends in life? To whom are we so thankful for sticking out her neck? Janie. She knew how to pursue a relationship (hey – they were skiing half the time!) but the clarity of the message of Christ was allowed to intrude at the appropriate times.

Kevin Ford, in his book *Jesus for a New Generation*, says, "It's not easy to reach my generation by arguing with them, but it is very easy to reach them by loving them, by sticking with them and standing by them, by helping them, by befriending them and letting them into your own life. My generation hungers for friends who will be loyal and genuine."[6] Or as Lynn Ellis of the Inter-Varsity missions division puts it, "I'm not an expert, but I'm a 27-year-old follower of Jesus Christ who believes that every human being is made in God's image, and that God has plans for every person and for every group of people, every

---

6 K. Ford *Jesus for a New Generation* (Downer's Grove: InterVarsity Press, 1995)

culture, every generation... I'm sick of hearing how desperate the situation seems. You'd think God went out of his way to form a generation whose passion it is to simply spend time with people. It takes a broken generation to reach a broken world." For this generation preaching means not how loud you can talk but how authentic your passion is.

I won't easily forget the lesson taught to me by V.J. Menon who was brought up as a Hindu and later chose to follow Christ and led others in the same path. His point was that true friendship involves being *loyal*. He put it this way: "Are you being my friend just because you want to tell me about Jesus, or are you telling me about Jesus because you want to be my friend?" That's a good test of the loyalty of our friendships.

Expect God to use you

The historical record in the New Testament ends with Paul having arrived in Rome. He has obviously looked forward to this day and the very last thing he says is, "God's salvation has been sent to the Gentiles, and they will listen."[7] He expected that God's word would do its work. He knew well the Old Testament promise in Isaiah where God says, "My word that goes out of my mouth ... will not return to me empty, but will accomplish what I desire."[8] We can and should expect God to use us too. Not everyone with whom you share your faith will be ready or willing to receive Christ. So when should I expect to see results? Not my business. Just remember that success in sharing your faith is simply taking the initiative to talk about Jesus Christ in the power of the Holy Spirit and leaving the results to God.

On a visit to Kerry my wife and I met a man we hadn't seen for years. We had known him as a student when he came to Bible discussions in our home. We were never sure whether he

---

7 Acts 28:28

8 Isaiah 55:11

had a grasp of what was going on. He would ask such obscure questions that meant he was either a genius beyond our level or the wheels had come off his understanding. When he was thinking (or whatever it was) he had the habit of preparing to light his pipe. He would drop in a piece of tobacco and then try to get it going with the stub of a match, which would fall in too. One evening our exasperated Bible study leader asked him, in some desperation, "I have only one question for you — are you smoking tobacco or matches?" We stayed good friends but he left the college and our contact quickly faded. Then fifteen years later he stood up at a Christian meeting, completely out of the blue and asked, "Do you know David Wilson?" Some of them did, which seemed to comfort him and encouraged him to keep talking. He then proceeded to tell them how God had followed his movements for all those intervening years, since the crazy days in our sitting room, and how he had brought him to faith, now as clear as a bell. God will look after results in his own good time.

Don't worry – the Holy Spirit has been using the witness of Christ's followers for two thousand years and he's all ready to use yours too. Success in sharing your faith is simply taking the initiative to talk about Jesus Christ in the power of the Holy Spirit and leaving the results to God. Expect God to use you.

Do the maths

It's hard to choose between the thrill of seeing God use you and that of seeing God use someone you coached. The first is addition, the second multiplication. I received a curious letter one autumn morning from a tax inspector (but not the kind of letter people normally get from them). He said that during the summer a local man, whom he had not previously known, came to visit him. In the course of their time together this man had advised the taxman on how to make a commitment to Christ, which he had now done. He wanted to know what he should he do next. He was 100 miles away so it was hard for me to say. I wrote back with cordial greetings and suggested that he would benefit from joining me and some others in learning how to share his new-found faith.

A couple of months later we all met up and took the sort of training outlined in this chapter. The taxman wasn't long home again when I received another letter – this time incandescent with delight. He had led their only son to Christ and was so emboldened by that experience he wanted to talk to anyone who was remotely interested. Since then he has not only been used to help to bring people to faith but to lead them towards maturity and has since taken on a key role with a missionary society. Which would you choose – guiding one person towards knowing God or training a guide who would influence the lives of many? Thankfully you don't have to choose – you can do both. And I want to suggest that indeed you do some of both.

Multiplication tables

Paul passed on his recipe for growth to his number one disciple, Timothy: "The things you have heard me say in the presence of many witnesses entrust to reliable men who will also be qualified to teach others."[9] Do you see the generations here? The first is Paul himself, then Timothy, then the "reliable" people, then the "others" that the reliable people will teach. If each reliable person had, say, four disciples (that's not too many is it?) and there were four reliable people (I don't know how many there were but three sounds a bit thin) we already have 18 people in this verse! But Paul made disciples throughout his life (I count 12 in the New Testament). If they were anything like Timothy (who was actually supposed to be a timid specimen) then in Paul's immediate circle there were over 200 on whose life he had an impact!

---

9   2 Timothy 2:2

You have a circle around you too. There is a unique sphere of influence of people whose lives you connect with. Nobody else has a circle like yours. God has hand-picked you to bring blessing and hope into their lives. Those in your circle probably consist of some believers and some unbelievers. We have already talked about choosing five to pray for who do not yet know Christ. Now I want you to think of five others who do know Christ and could use help, encouragement and a little training so they can, in turn, change their world. You could start by praying for them and lending them this book. Browse through the list of resources at the end of the book and see which of them would be a good boost for the witness of your friends. Join with one or two others and each of you share your 'Five in Focus' so you can pray and work together and support each other.

Ever thought of being a big-time missionary? OK, maybe not. But do you know what good missionaries do? They do exactly what you are doing if you have followed the pointers in these last two chapters. You can go to bed at night knowing you have fulfilled part of God's world plan for that day. That's destiny in anybody's book!

CHAPTER 8

WORLDWIDE NET

We have already seen that the scope of God's thinking is big-hearted. It's global. This is an enterprise in which each of us can be involved. It's fair to ask: "Why?"

Reasons

For starters, God is not willing that anyone should perish.[1] Peter says that's why Jesus has not come back for us just yet. He's not slow – just patient (which is a completely different thing). In the meantime "Christ's love compels us"[2] – it pulls us along. Haven't you ever had the feeling about somebody you know and respect, "Wouldn't it be great if they could know Christ! Their life wouldn't frustrate them any more and they'd be fulfilled." There are people around you, even the happy, shiny ones, who have an ache in their hearts for reconciliation with God – "and he has committed to us the message of reconciliation."[3] What a luxury! We come on as good news. I mean, we can say with authority, "Everything's going to turn out all right. Relax – you don't need to worry your head about making an out-of-court settlement with God. It's been taken care of. Somebody has paid – and I have the receipt here for you, if you'd just like to sign ..."

People are hungry. Throughout the first century the gospel message met and satisfied the heart-hunger for God in a widely diverse set of cultures. This has continued down the centuries and our century is no exception. Changes in the fortunes of organised religion still leave the rough, parched tongue of human thirst for God and spiritual things. As Sinéad O'Connor once said in an interview with the *Times*, "I always knew that God was there despite religion, and I've always been interested in rescuing God from religion."[4]

---

1   2 Peter 3:9

2   2 Corinthians 5:14

3   2 Corinthians 5:19

4   N. Williamson *The Times* July 1, 2000 The Times / NI Syndication

And people are also lost. It broke Jesus' heart to be around people who were lost and couldn't see it. It drove him to tears. One of his longest stories was about lostness (Luke chapter 15). In the story of the missing sheep his heart shows. A man has 100 sheep. One goes missing so he leaves the 99 (like you do) and spends his energies on the missing one until he finds it. But you *don't* leave 99 sheep to the mercies of the elements and wildlife. The man's mind was snagged on the lostness of the one. The story of life doesn't end there. In Hebrews we are reminded that "man is destined to die once, and after that to face judgement."[5] Following Christ is not just a lifestyle choice. Let's pray that God will let us see those around us through Jesus' eyes.

The one towering reason must surely be the care with which Christ commissioned his disciples with their life's assignment, documented in the New Testament five times. Let's consider that Great Commission carefully – I get the impression from Acts chapter one that they talked about it for six weeks!

Who gave the Great Commission?

In the account in Matthew Jesus starts off by saying, "All authority in heaven and on earth has been given to me."[6] This was not just to remind them who he was, but what they would be when they went out in this venture representing him. They would have all the authority they ever needed because it derived from Jesus Christ who had stared death in the face – and won. He had seen around every corner of the darkness of human nature – and paid the price. He had left Satan with a permanent and fatal bruise on his head. He had seen off the strenuous attempts of the world's best professional killers to keep him dead. During these last transitional weeks with them he had even reproduced one of his earliest miracles, a massive catch of fish, to remind them that he is Lord over all creation and to concentrate the mind, one more time, on fishing. Fishing for men, that is.

---

5 Hebrews 9:27
6 Matthew 28:18-20

"As the Father has sent me, I am sending you,"[7] Jesus tells the disciples towards the end of his time on earth with them. He wastes no time in getting around to this subject. He has just appeared on resurrection day in the upstairs room where the disciples were hiding and all he has said so far is, "Peace be with you." So how did the Father send the Son? Luke gives us an answer: "The Son of Man came to seek and save what was lost."[8] Now his plan is to continue to seek and save the lost through you! This is the hour for which you were born. If you feel inadequate you're in good company – the eleven men listening to Jesus did not yet know what to make of it. But expressing his love and forgiveness to the world through the lives of changed people was God's plan A and there isn't a plan B – not then, not now. Christ's full authority has been vested in plan A.

So we have the right to pass on the message about God's love to anyone. Sometimes we talk about 'earning the right to be heard,' meaning that an insensitive attitude to other people will be a right turn-off. But strictly speaking, we already have every right to talk to everyone. This may be more important than you think, even in simple matters like when you ask yourself, "Who am I to approach this person? Maybe the gospel is an imposition on their time and their life?" No, it isn't. Feel free to proceed. Because you will also find, as they did in the first century, that God has got there before you to prepare people. Psalm 19 tells us that we will find people have already learned some things about God purely from seeing the skies above them. In Romans we see those who do not yet know God learning about "his eternal power and divine nature"[9] from the natural world around them. Paul and Barnabas met a group (the Lycaonians) who had already experienced God's kindness through, amongst other things, *joie*

---

[7] John 20:21

[8] Luke 19:10

[9] Romans 1:20

de vivre![10] Paul and Barnabas weren't going around looking for miserable people to share the gospel with. They talked to anything that moved and God saw to it that they ran into those he had already been drawing to himself.

Georgia, a friend of ours at University College Dublin, made the acquaintance of a student who had recently returned from Paris. Pretty soon Georgia told her about her faith in Christ and the student came to accept Christ without much further ado. Then she told us a remarkable story. She had been brought up in Dublin in a well-ordered and well-educated family with the normal dose of religious heritage. She decided that she wanted to escape from God and so left to study in Paris (thinking that God lived in Ireland). Walking along the banks of the Seine she saw (just like in the movies) young couples sitting together holding hands, embracing, madly in love. Something snapped within her and she said, "There must be a God!" She packed up and came home to find God. But where to look? Within a week she had met Georgia and found the final piece to her puzzle – God had been looking for her. And what about Georgia? Had she been looking for someone with 'Potential Christian' embroidered on their back-pack?! No, Georgia had simply been obedient to pass on what God had given her to those he brought her into contact with. That's why he gets called "the Lord of the Harvest" in the gospels. He has a masterful way of working things out to gather in the crop of lost people he has already paid for. He's got the authority. You can use it. You're licensed to talk to anybody who will listen. Even if there were no other reason to take the Great Commission seriously, one would remain – for the honour of Christ.

---

10 Acts 14:17

To whom was the Great Commission given?

It was going to be twelve men but, as you know, Judas didn't make it. That left eleven. (After the Ascension the disciples selected another twelfth man.) What made the initial numbers less important was the way this commission was to be passed on to others. Everyone who accepted the apostles' message received, in his or her own turn, the exact same assignment. The Lord expressed it like this: "Go and make disciples, teaching them to obey everything I have commanded you," which of course included this commission itself. This has now come down to us. On one of RTE's remarkable documentaries I heard an old man say, "There are only twenty-five old men between you and Jesus Christ!" Over those years many have risked and lost their lives to hand on the baton intact. This also means that when you coach those whom God has given you to disciple, you want to be careful to pass on the whole assignment to them.

A spiritual generation doesn't need to take as long as a biological generation. Take Declan, for example. He grew up in Armagh. He ended up working in a computer assembly plant in Galway alongside John who shared his interest in playing good guitar. John was a believer in Christ which Declan noticed fairly soon because you couldn't miss it. John took flak from colleagues for reading the Bible at lunchtime. At first Declan only felt pity for John but soon felt inexorably drawn to make his own commitment to Christ. Now, John was himself a new believer because he had met up with Bernie, a girl he had known at school, who returned home at the university half-term break and told him she had come to faith and it was the greatest thing since sliced bread. Bernie had gone to university with a sunny disposition and a passion for sport. In her first term she met Laurie who was full of beans and ready to explain why to anybody. That's four spiritual generations in the space of a couple of years. The trick is to make sure that Christ's commission is passed on.

About a dozen of us were taking the ferry from Dover to Calais when Thera, one of our number, chatted on the ferry with a travelling middle-aged lady who had a rich husband and an expensive taste in fur coats. They talked about this husband's business, which happened to be in electronics and then, to save the conversation from one-sidedness, the lady asked, "And what do you do?" "I'm one of twelve of us on this boat," said Thera, "and we're all personal servants of one man." Now the woman's eyes were like saucers. "I didn't know there was much of that kind of thing any more!" she said, trying to get her head around what it must be like in the sumptuous mansion where we undoubtedly worked. "We're all servants of Jesus Christ," Thera chirped up. As if this little talk weren't unusual enough already, the world traveller then began to cry. She had had the chance to become a "personal servant of Jesus Christ" when she was in her late teens and had turned it down! The sheer elegance of Thera's authority had brought her up short and reminded her of what she thought was a chance lost and gone forever. Thera, of course, being a proper servant of Jesus, took the opportunity to explain that God is the God of the second chance. So Christ's commission passes to a new generation, courtesy of people like Thera, you and me.

What is involved in the Great Commission?

The scope of the Lord's plan included giving every person on earth a chance to hear about him and the privilege of learning how to follow him. It was not an information campaign but rather had the purpose of seeing whole groups of people, not just individuals, changed by following Christ. The past twenty centuries have seen his radical effect in the lives of those who follow him, to the extent that whole societies have had to take Christ seriously because the change is so significant. For example, a politician whose life was defined by following Christ was William Wilberforce. He introduced an anti slave-trade motion in the British House of Commons in 1788 concluding, "Sir, when we think of eternity and the future consequence of all human conduct, what is there in this life that shall make any man contradict the dictates of his conscience, the principles of justice and the law of God!"[11] The motion was defeated. Nobody much noticed. It was a non-runner. He brought it up again every year for the next eighteen years until it was passed. William Wilberforce then spent the rest of his life working against slavery itself. It was outlawed a month after his death in 1833.

As we see Christ's commission obeyed in our time we too can look forward to our culture sitting up and taking notice of who he is. I can't wait. The air is full of expectations as people talk about 'ethics,' the 'spiritual,' 'authentic relationships,' 'justice,' 'evil,' 'equality,' 'partnership' with developing countries. These are now dearly held values but for many people they are almost devoid of content. As more and more people turn to Christ, learn his new life and see it reproduced inside them through the Holy Spirit, our society will get an opportunity to see, close up, how these same values can be practised in high-definition detail.

The world-wide mission of Christ is not the same as social reform. It aims first at spiritual renewal, but social reform is then to be expected. Thus it was that spiritually changed individuals first worked against the caste system in India in the nineteenth century, introduced the first universities in China at the beginning of the twentieth century, began the Red Cross, convened the Geneva convention, pioneered literacy world-wide, founded the first trade unions, and an encyclopaedia of other issues. So why isn't the world saved forever yet? Because despite the significant change seen in the lives of Christ's followers, others do not want him running their lives and are prepared to see more of man's inhumanity to man instead. The next item on the agenda, once the gospel has been spread everywhere, is Christ's return to stage the biggest sort-out the world has ever seen.

---

11 E. Metaxas *Amazing Grace: William Wilberforce and the Heroic Campaign to End Slavery* (Oxford: Monarch, 2007), 231

Meanwhile you can be a key player in our century by being a part of this greatest challenge ever issued by the greatest person who ever lived. Part of that challenge is to make sure nobody gets left out. Imagine waking up in the morning and finding that the whole world around you had heard the story of Jesus. Impossible? It's not only possible but it has already happened – in AD 60. When the apostle Paul wrote a letter to his contacts in Turkey he said, "This gospel is bearing fruit and growing all over the world."[12] Before you say, "He would, wouldn't he," remember that this growth of the gospel had gone into every quarter of the Roman Empire in three decades flat, against all the odds. They had to deal with logistical difficulties hard for us to imagine. (Paul was literally in chains in a Roman prison and this letter had to be dictated.) The story of Jesus was getting to be general knowledge. Indeed three years earlier he wrote to the friends in Rome before he ever got there himself and told them that he had explained the gospel "from Jerusalem all the way round to Illyricum" (Albania!).[13]

Now it's our turn! If ever there was a time for us to release the information about Jesus into the public domain it is now. Let's give this century a good boost with a decent chance to get the story straight about Jesus.

Where does the Great Commission apply?

When Jesus announced the task of reaching every 'nation' he wasn't thinking of nations as we know them today – like Brazil, Germany or Zimbabwe. Our modern idea of nations as political units only got going properly after the Napoleonic wars. Jesus meant something deeper. The Bible word for 'nation' or 'people-groups' is deeper. It is like our word 'ethnic' and meant those people who get together around a common heritage, race, culture,

---

12 Colossians 1:6

13 Romans 15:19

religion and especially a common language. It's not that long ago (the 1990s) since Macedonia, Croatia, Bosnia, Herzegovina, Montenegro, Slovenia were all one 'country' (Yugoslavia) which then separated out into the various people-groups with startling speed when Yugoslavia was no more.

So when we think of the 'Irish' people, they aren't just people who live in Ireland – some live in London, Birmingham, Boston and Australia. Kurdish people live in Iran, Iraq, Turkey and now, in Germany. And we have 'new Irish' people living in Ireland! So although there are practising Christians in more or less every country (political unit) in the world we can approach the task more accurately by asking, "Which people-groups have sustainable groups of believers praising God in their own language?" Sociologists have counted about 16,500 'peoples.' Around 9,500 of these have organised Christian communities. This is up from twenty years ago, which makes this a time when history is being made. This leaves us with around 7,000 'people-groups' who have yet to understand the gospel in their own culture.[14] Of course it's not a bad idea to organise for a whole country to hear the gospel – usually you will need to break it down into people-groups at some stage if nobody is going to be left out.

No stone was left unturned when the Lord Jesus spelled out the geography. At the beginning of the Book of Acts he specifies, "You will be my witnesses in Jerusalem, and in all Judea and Samaria [this bit was conceivable, even though it wasn't easy] and to the ends of the earth" (off the screen for the average disciple).[15] Nobody was as surprised as those same disciples when, lo and behold, one after another the Lord's targets were reached! But the disciples didn't wait for everything in Jerusalem to work out just fine before they took on further vistas of challenge. The same sweep of geography beckons us now in our time. We have already

---

14 Statistics from www.joshuaproject.net accessed May 2013
15 Acts 1:8

talked about being effective witnesses in our own backyard, which is always the way to start, but the call of the wild also beckons. Likewise you can allow yourself to get interested in how God could use you further afield while you are still being faithful to your friends locally. "Jerusalem – Judea – Samaria – earthsend" wasn't meant to be always done in strict rotation.

People of non-Christian background are often spoken of as if they were not in the 'market share' of the Christian God. There is no such person as the 'Christian God.' There is one God and he sends his love to absolutely anyone. It would be nice if we could learn to be as generous. In Romans Paul remarks that "The gospel is the power of God for the salvation of everyone who believes: first for the Jew, then for the Gentile."[16] What he meant by "the Gentiles," of course, was the rest of us! We mustn't lose our nerve at this point and think that the power of God only extends to those in our people-group, just because it is so familiar to us. There are aspects of the gospel which are especially applicable to people of other groups. We only learn the extent of that gospel by sharing it and watching it work.

What's already been done in the Great Commission?

The story so far is that there are at least a million Bible-believing people in most countries of the world. This did not happen by accident. I never fail to be enchanted by the stories of those who have gone before us in making Christ known to a burning world.

For example, Henry Grattan Guinness (grandson of Arthur Guinness), born in Dublin in 1835, became a key player in worldwide mission by setting up missionary training, first in Dublin, later in London. In the process he founded three whole missionary societies as well as training over a thousand students. When he was setting up in Dublin his first student was Thomas

---

16 Romans 1:16

Barnardo, who went on to found 'Barnardo's' which is today a major provider of programmes to help children and families in Ireland and a leading UK children's charity.[17]

Those turn-of-the-last-century missionaries were spunky people. In 1885 students at Dublin University (Trinity College) set up their own mission (the D.U. Mission) through which graduates were sent, especially to India and China. One of the many from Dublin was Samuel Synge, doctor and a brother of John Millington Synge, who went to China in 1896 and weathered the storm of the Boxer rebellion in 1900 alongside Chinese Christians who suffered for their faith.

When you choose to obey Christ's commission you follow in noble footsteps. One place you can almost hear those footsteps is in the entrance to Trinity College, just inside the Front Gate. As you proceed inside the archway you will notice framed wooden notice boards along the walls. They are reserved for the notices of the various clubs and societies, each of which have a discreetly painted name. One of those on the right still has the faded name "D.U. Mission."

Another place with noble footsteps is down the street and round the corner on Eden Quay, for it was there that Eva Stuart Watt and her sister Clara set out to help city centre people find peace in Christ in the 1940s. Eva wrote that it started one evening,

> "after midnight when, walking up Grafton Street, we met a lovely girl. We told her that God wanted her to come back to him. 'I?' she exclaimed rather startled, stepping back against the shop window to face us. 'I've gone too far!' As we accompanied her down the partially lighted street, she looked this way and that way like a frightened bird. 'All the police recognize me,' she said. Then came the story we all know so well, of womanhood – childhood in this case – sacrificed on the altar of vice."[18]

---

[17] M. Guinness *Genius of Guinness* (Greenville, Belfast: Ambassador, 2005), 65

[18] E. Stuart Watt *Ireland Awakening* (Chicago: Moody Press, 1952), 20

Then, a few lines further in her account, Eva simply says, "We kissed her." That attitude of radical Christian compassion exemplified Eva and Clara's work. They recalled meeting "a tall handsome young fellow in evening dress, with a beautiful girl leaning on each arm...What touched him seemingly was the hour they were being spoken to, two-thirty in the morning."[19] That was normal for the Stuart Watts because that's when they could meet the most people with the most needs. "Another morning we dropped into the Colburn Café in Marlboro Street for a hot drink just before closing hour, 4:00 A.M."; "About 2:00 A.M. one summer Sunday morning in O'Connell Street" they met "a young chap, shivering and unshaven."

They describe a visit to an "all-night drinking den" at one o'clock in the morning. With the permission of the manager of this shebeen/brothel they distributed Christian literature and the New Testament and invited some of the clients around to their flat "for a cup of tea" (now at two o'clock in the morning!). This 'flat' where they lived in frugality was a tiny place near Busaras which was just then being built.

They wrote most of the leaflets they distributed (by the thousand) around the city centre. In one of these, "Blood In The History of Ireland", they quote from Wolfe Tone, Robert Emmet and from Thomas McDonagh's address to the court martial that sentenced him to death. McDonagh salutes his hero, the 15th century Savonarola, "whose weapon was not the sword, but prayer and preaching." Eva even writes about the "future history of Ireland" which is to "influence the world." *"Henceforth we are missionaries or we are nothing!"* "The gates are even now ajar for a great moral and spiritual awakening, that could bless humanity far beyond the limit of our shores."[20]

Many have come and gone and served with distinction since Eva and Clara but the work of Teen Challenge reminds me of

---

19 Stuart Watt (1952,22)

20 Stuart Watt (1952,101-103)

them a bit. It's back in Marlboro Street, back to help addicts, back to midnight, back to bring the gospel to the neediest. When President Michael D. Higgins opened their new centre for women at Tiglin, County Wicklow, in 2012 he remarked that "Teen Challenge in Ireland started out as an outreach team serving those affected by homelessness, drug and alcohol addiction."[21]

I'm sure that you, like me, regard these historical greats with awe. But we don't live in the nineteenth or twentieth centuries. To look at the task that still remains we now need to think strategically about people-groups. That was how the book of Acts unfolded as Paul visited Athens (chapter 17) and explained the message to them with painstaking care. He was acutely conscious that he was standing at the centre of the Greek-speaking world. Two chapters later he says, "I must visit Rome also."[22] He wasn't thinking about the architecture – he was dreaming wild dreams of seeing God's gospel planted at the heart of the Roman empire. From there it would be carried along naturally on the waves of human migration since all roads led away from Rome as well as to it.

I met a young man from a Buddhist/Taoist background when he was studying on a campus near where we lived. Somehow I had assumed he was a Christian but as we got to know each other better on a weekend away he explained that he was not. He didn't know how his family would take it if he accepted Christ and he wanted to be loyal to them. I asked if he had considered that God had a better plan for his family than he even had himself. Maybe he was the obstacle to that blessing and all heaven could break loose if he would make the first move. After spending the weekend in the company of Christians from a variety of non-Christian backgrounds he went back to his Hall of Residence and invited Christ to come into his life. Later he wrote, "I was consoled in a way knowing that I was not alone and God will help

---

21 www.president.ie/speeches/1521-2 accessed May 2013

22 Acts 19:21

me overcome adversities...So on that fateful night I accepted Christ into my life...God has extended his hand and I have held it. In the past I was blind and ignorant, but the moment I was interested God opened the floodgate and engulfed me with the overwhelming truth."

Some friends at a Russian university introduced me to a young woman who was following one of the new mystical religions. Because we might both be liable to misunderstand some of the spiritual terms we were using, we went over everything very carefully. After a long discussion she said she was not quite ready to receive Christ into her life – she felt "very guilty," although she wouldn't be specific. A couple of days later she found an old church building (not always easy to do in her circumstances!) and chose to pray to receive Christ in that setting. It turned out that she had struggled with depression. A year-and-a-half previously her only daughter had died, aged 14 months, having been misdiagnosed. After only a few weeks as a new person in Christ she sent me a message to say she was "experiencing Jesus as the gentle Shepherd." We sometimes forget how magnetically attractive is the person of Christ when really understood and encountered for the first time.

What's left to do in the Great Commission?

Around 7,000 or so people-groups have yet to hear the gospel clearly. The great majority of these groups are Muslim, animist, Hindu or Buddhist. Priority deserves to be given to those who are at the greatest distance socially, culturally and linguistically. That priority, in increasing order of need, would be: (a) a person in your district who occasionally attends church. This person lives in a culture which has been reached with Christ's message – they just haven't responded; (b) someone in your district with another religious background, or no background. You still share some of their social environment and you could get in touch with them – your bins are collected by the same lorry and your mail is delivered by the same postman; (c) someone of another background whose living conditions ensure that they are most unlikely to meet Christians and make any sense of them. You don't know this person and neither do I. It just so happens that they make up the majority of the unreached people-groups and they aren't going to hear unless somebody somewhere breaks the rules – those rules of social convention that keep us distant from those who could benefit from our company. Feel in the mood to break a few rules? There is no special office to which eccentric Christians apply who want to work on this venture. It is all done by people like you. Yes, really, people like you.

There are four valuable assets that make it easier to be involved in reaching new people-groups. These are: the ability to speak one of the worldwide languages; the use of a currency which can be traded internationally; universal access to education, and automatic and easy access to a passport. Only a handful of countries have all four and Ireland is one of them. In the next section we will talk about how we can use these assets to the best advantage.

When I was visiting friends who live in central Russia I went to the local branch of the federal government to register my visit (this is the Russian way). Sitting in the same waiting room was a man from the Tatar group, a large Muslim minority in Russia. The only language we shared was schoolboy German. I think we were both fascinated by each other. In answering his barrage of questions I began to go through an explanation of how to come to God. After a little while he signalled energetically for me to stop and then apologised profusely for taking up my time, since I had obviously not understood that he was a Muslim and so the whole story didn't apply to him – Jesus would doubtless love Christians (since they belonged to Jesus' group) but Muslims were a different matter. I then had the privilege of showing him that John 3:16 does not say that God loved Christians so much that he gave his one and only Son, but rather that he also loved Muslims equally, since it says that he loved the whole world. This was a revelation to him and a thrill for me to be the first ever person to explain to him God's feelings for Muslims.

Making the best use of your assets

This book has already given you all the vital ingredients you need to engage in Christ's commission. Maybe you will also have the opportunity to cross over cultural lines to communicate Christ to those who are disadvantaged by reason of their life's circumstances. But 'learn the trade' in your own language in your own culture first. Make your early mistakes with us! Then when you have the basics practised thoroughly enough you can move on. That way God will deal with issues in your life that are close to you because you process them in your mother tongue and you will have something to say when people of another culture ask if you have applied this spiritual remedy to your own culture.

You know more about other cultures than you think. You don't need a holiday abroad to follow the news of conflict or environmental issues in other countries. Maybe you travel in connection with your work or study or you follow sporting fixtures played in international venues. Perhaps you have family or close friends who live in a different country in a different culture. There is a rich well of cultural information right there on the tip of your tongue. This will help you pray for people-groups who currently haven't a hope of hearing about Christ. As you pray and ask God how you can serve him in this way he will impress you with more specific issues to pray for and he will lead you to ways you can be directly involved.

There are many opportunities to start small with a try-out by going short-term to work in a spiritually needy culture. Choose a project that gives you direct interaction with people in the new culture. Why not go with somebody else you know and join a team? It's more fun that way and you will be able to compare notes and get more good out of the learning experience. Stay in touch with those you meet in that culture (and that team) and soon you will be setting your sights on other horizons with longer term choices.

When you are ready to invest part of your life in cross-cultural mission, put enough time into training. God does not regard this as a 'rush job' and neither should we (training stands you in good stead for life anyway). Whatever you do, include (a) sufficient Bible knowledge; (b) fluency in how to lead someone to put their faith in Christ, how to follow up those that do and how to follow up those that don't; (c) cross-cultural communication.

Move it

And while we're talking about spiritually needy cultures – what are we going to do about this one in which God has placed us? Our people have known the main elements of the Christian faith for over 1500 years. But recently they have been forgetting. How can we see to it that everyone in this little country has a chance to hear how to come to know God personally? How can we plant the seed of the gospel at the heart of Irish culture so that it is unmistakable, unavoidable, like switching on a new floodlight to re-energise a tired old game? Is there anything we can do? Yes, there is everything!

Keeping your allegiance to present Christ to the people of your own locality is of paramount importance, but I want to encourage you also to "Think broad – act local." It is such a massive encouragement to hear what others in our culture are doing, to pray for them, co-operate with them, learn from them. Only by planning and working together will we see the commission of Christ fulfilled in our own country, but as we work together under God's guidance it *will* be fulfilled. I want to be part of that enterprise! Will you join the undertaking to ensure that we include every man, woman and child in Ireland? Every school, university, factory, office, hospital, company, government department, neighbourhood. We won't want to leave anybody out. Sound like a tall order? Here's the good news. God has his people absolutely everywhere and they are in a mood to co-operate as never before. This is an ultimately high purpose that gives all believers enough common ground to work shoulder to shoulder.

There's always a special magic in the air when a whole group, neighbourhood or a company reaches 'saturation.' Unbelievers talk to other unbelievers about Christ – a sure sign that the gospel is going public.

Find a few others where you work, live or study who will join you to pray for the acquaintances in your immediate surroundings. Have a brainstorm together to answer the question, "What would it take for all of our people to understand the gospel to the point where they could respond?" Don't let go of the aim of letting everyone hear.

Golden opportunity

The Lord of the harvest has entrusted to us in Ireland a special opportunity for local involvement that brings blessing far beyond our local community – we are hosts to a growing immigrant population from various places around the world. Local government can't always be expected to know how best to help immigrants, but we can take our cue from God's instruction to the Israelites: "When an alien lives with you in your land, do not ill-treat him. The alien living with you must be treated as one of your native-born. Love him as yourself, for you were aliens in Egypt. I am the Lord your God."[23]

You may already know where there are immigrants in your district who need assistance integrating into Irish culture. If not,

---

23 Leviticus 19:33

you can volunteer even a little time by contacting the local council office who will usually be glad for the help. You can guarantee that your new neighbours will never forget their first months in Ireland. You can make it a pleasant memory for people who will say ever after, "When the chips were down, the Christians helped us." Some immigrants are themselves believers who, as our brothers and sisters, need to be treated like family. This is not just because we belong to Jesus together but because they will have something from their walk with God to teach us.

I owe you one

Here's one final motivation to help us look at people differently. We owe them the gospel – that's right, we owe them! This remarkable idea comes in Romans chapter 1 where Paul says "I am bound [literally, 'I am a debtor'] both to Greeks and non-Greeks, both to the wise and the foolish. That is why I am so eager to preach the gospel to you who are at Rome."[24]

If I meet you one day and I give you five Euro to pass on to a mutual friend, you will then say to the friend the next time you meet them, "I owe you five Euro." They may well say, "No, I think you're mistaken; you don't owe me anything." But of course you do. At that point you need to back up and explain to the friend that I had asked you to pass it on and therefore the fiver isn't yours, you really do owe it to them.

So one good reason why I want to introduce the Lord to more new people is because I owe them! God has loved me intensely and more than I need actually. The extra was given to me to pass on. Whether you realise it or not, you have received the greatest commission from the greatest Person. We have been handed the torch of gospel light by valiant people in the twentieth century. Christ is still the one with the authority in the twenty-first century. Let's make the most of it!

---

24 Romans 1:14

CHAPTER 9

LEADERSHIP

If you have recently become a Christian you may well be wondering what you are doing reading a chapter like this. Surely leadership is for the connected, the up-front types, the mind-readers, the beautiful, the seriously trained? Read on.

Maybe you have already seen in yourself a spark of ability and readiness to lead. But where can you get advice? Well, there is no scarcity of books being published on the subject. Take, for example, the selection of titles in an airport bookshop. Along with the light holiday reading there are always shelves full of books on leadership and management. Most fall into two categories: (a) Throw your weight around and (b) Throw your weight around while pretending to be interested in other people. The end goal of such leadership is a healthy financial bottom line. In a new variant the goal is self-actualisation – so long as there is a healthy financial bottom line. Anything seem peculiar about this picture of leadership?

Dual citizenship

It certainly seemed peculiar to Jesus who, when he was outlining the arrangements for leading, took on the airport books head-on: "The kings of the Gentiles lord it over them; and those who exercise authority over them call themselves Benefactors. But you are not to be like that. Instead the greatest among you should be like the youngest, and the one who rules like the one who serves."[1] Then, in case the disciples were thinking, "But this is the way the whole world is run – are we going to be able to swing it all around to be different?" the Lord went on to say, "I confer on you a kingdom, just as my Father conferred one on me."[2] Jesus was beginning a new kingdom, which is now already running, of which you and I are a part. We live in two kingdoms at once, and they are run by very different rules.

---

1 Luke 22:25,26
2 Luke 22:29

To get people to do things using the old kingdom rules, you "lord it over them", as Jesus put it. You have authority, wherever you got it from, and you apply it to others in some form of "Do this or else." Both stick and carrot are available to you in old kingdom methods. The carrot element, on which Jesus commented, is patronage – being a "benefactor," becoming the single supplier to someone to the point where they are obliged to work for you. In Matthew he tells you how it is done – a lot of it has to do with outward appearances: the power icons of how you dress, your public profile, your title.[3] These two great worldly-wise methods, power and patronage, are ruled out at a stroke by Jesus' statement: "You are not to be like that."

Your serve

So how do things work according to new kingdom rules? Very differently. Even the end goal is different because we work so that God gets the credit. And the way leaders conduct themselves is to be different too. The ones who are running things are to be like waiters serving tables![4] The greatest should be like the youngest – not 'young' in the sense of childish, but without an automatic 'right to rule.' If you feel like a junior person, if you are on the lower rungs of the ladder, then you are in good company. That's where people are supposed to get to in order to start leading. You are there already! Christian leading involves having a servant mindset because you are not working on your own terms. Those who take on the mantle of leading in God's kingdom always know there is Someone to Whom they themselves must report. That should help them keep things in perspective.

It has often been said that your servant attitude is never more severely tested than when someone actually treats you like a servant. But what if you actually wanted to be a servant in the

---

[3] Matthew 23:5-12

[4] Luke 22:27

first place? Sometimes I think of this in the supermarket when buying a grocery item that says, right there on the packaging, 'serves two,' or four, or whatever. If your aim is to be a servant then your serving capacity is what you would want to measure. In the glorious upside-down world of God's kingdom that is a key parameter: "How many do I serve?" Not "How many people am I in charge of?" Servant leadership is a relationship. Parading your power isn't.

Professional servant

One's serving capacity is shown at odd times – unplanned – like when somebody intrudes into my space and time and agenda with a need that I can best meet. Is it my knee-jerk reaction to say "Great! I'm a professional servant and you're going to make my day complete because you are providing me with an extra and unusual opportunity to do what I'm made for – serving"? I mean, if you are selling double-glazing, the more homes you glaze the more successful you are. And if you're a servant you're always looking out for further chances to serve more people, better. You'll always find enough service opportunities around you in the form of people – that is God's way. But as Paul told the Colossians, ultimately "It is the Lord Christ you are serving."[5]

Each of the authors of the New Testament letters introduce themselves at some point as 'servants.' No wonder. Jesus had said, "Whoever serves me must follow me; and where I am, my servant also will be. My Father will honour the one who serves me."[6] If you begin to think of serving him as your occupation a lot of things become clear. I pray I never get so clever at time management that I fail to hear, "Well done, good and faithful servant."[7] Believe me – if and when I ever hear those words I'll go round heaven like we just won the cup.

---

5 Colossians 3:24

6 John 12:26

7 Matthew 25:21

Leadership ideas from the old kingdom die hard and we are much more deeply imprinted with them than we think. I believe this is why Jesus went into some detail about how the old kingdom works – just so we know the ideologies we're up against, not only in the world around us, but in our own thinking. When the two worlds collide, which you may often find happening at your place of work, for example, try the Lord's Golden Rule: "Do to others what you would have them do to you."[8] When you are leading others that will sort out a lot of the questions that arise.

Leading roles

You may still be wondering if you are 'cut out' to be a leader. Relax. There is no such thing as a leadership gene. Although popular culture thinks of 'born leaders' who can do everything, this is extremely unusual. There is a range of different roles to be taken on by a leader and some can take on particular roles better than others. These include the direction-setter, the change agent, the coach, the spokesperson and the steward.

The direction-setter is the person who comes up with the bright ideas and says, "Let's all go in this direction!" They don't mind standing up in front of other people to say why their idea is a good one. They are not easily swayed by what everybody else thinks either. This inspirational role is the most famous part of leadership because it is the most visible.

But soon another role is needed – that of the change agent. This is where the leader needs to get into more details, helping others own the new idea, taking questions, coming up with solutions together, putting in the time and energy. This is a stage we can't do without.

Then there is the coach. This is the role part played by the leader to help each player on the team play to their best potential and not run out of gas. The leader will coax them, encourage them,

---

[8] Matthew 7:12

cajole them, show them how if necessary, and sincerely convince them that they are valued and that they can finish the task. The dream which the direction-setter came up with still needs to be kept alive. By this time the leader may well need to do some work as a spokesperson to those outside the immediate sphere of work, to promote understanding and to recruit resources.

Another responsibility of any leader of others is to be a steward – the trustee of the assigned resources. As a leader your 'top' resources (although that is rather too cold a word) will often be the people closest to you – family members or colleagues whom you might be tempted to take for granted. When you are also given responsibility to look after money you will want to make sure it is handled completely above board.

Who can juggle all these roles in perfect balance? Nobody I know. That's why the New Testament encourages leaders to work in a team context. Indeed when you come across a leader who is a one-man-band a little red light ought to go on in your head. Remember Jesus' words, "Apart from me you can do nothing" (John 15:5)? This applies to leading as much as anything else. God is the one leading his people and we are just servants in that process.

Heart trouble

Leadership is mainly an issue of the heart, not just a matter of getting the roles right. This is most clearly seen when things go wrong. Tell-tale weaknesses will show that all is not well. The leader may be too much of a perfectionist to be able to delegate jobs to other people. There will be a lack of transparency, maybe because they haven't kept up transparency in their relationship with God. Nobody can find out what direction the project is going in! They become unapproachable – because nobody wants their head bitten off. There are areas you can't touch because they will explode. Lack of self-control, especially the control of their tongue, becomes a problem. They lose the trust of those they wanted to lead. Maybe their integrity slips. Sometimes this will result in a leader being more noisy because they have become insecure. If the leader's trouble is in the heart that's where we will find the solutions too.

Keeping your heart

Back in chapter three we talked about 'spiritual breathing' – allowing God to fill us with his Spirit moment by moment, while we confess our sin and appreciate his forgiveness. If ever you needed spiritual breathing you need it now if you are going to be a leader. The Holy Spirit brings wisdom – something which you are going to be thankful for. Following Jesus puts you into the people-business and people put you into the problem-business and the problems pop up without time for you to get ready. They come unfiltered, untidy and raw. The best way to be prepared is to stay prepared, keeping "in step with the Spirit". When you need wisdom, just ask – "If any of you lacks wisdom, he should ask God, who gives generously to all without finding fault, and it will be given to him."[9] Now that's a relief, isn't it?

Here's another reason why your heart needs to remain sensitive: leaders have more faults to confess than others because they have more, not less, temptation. In Titus 1:7 Paul lists the qualities you don't want to find in a leader and top of the list is "overbearing." After years in Christian leadership, Thomas Abraham, originally from India, spoke about the temptations facing leaders. He said, "There are three famous temptations – money, sex and power. But there is an important fourth – getting to the stage where you trample over other people and say, 'I've been at this so long now I can do it whatever way I like.'" I found this to be a profound observation – from someone who had served Christ full-time for 30 years. Don't let leadership grow on you so that you love it more than the people you lead and the Lord whom you want to serve with integrity.

---
9   James 1:5

Audience of One

They say that the ultimate test of a gentleman is whether he uses a butter knife when there is no one else in the house. The test of a leader is how he or she performs when there is no one else watching them. This is the very opposite of the Pharisees who did everything to be seen by others. Our guiding principle is found in Colossians: "Whatever you do, work at it with all your heart, as working for the Lord, not for men, since you know that you will receive an inheritance from the Lord as a reward."[10] For a couple of years I was responsible for a human resources department and, upon leaving, had the task of shredding records that were of no further use. This was a strange day full of wistful memories of people who had passed through our hands during that time. The fattest files were about those who had problems which we worked to solve and contain. They were often the people who resigned in the end, who never became part of our success story. By my reckoning 80% of the bulk of the files were of this type and it made me think, "Did I spend 80% of that time with nothing to show for it?" Then I remembered whom I was really working for. It was precisely those tough decisions made in private that would test my mettle and be God's measure of my leadership. It is the audience of One that matters. "Your Father, who sees what is done in secret, will reward you."[11]

Don't lose heart

Not everybody is ready to respond to the gospel, no matter how good the news is. This can get you down – it certainly bothered the apostle Paul who said that this gave him a "great sorrow in my heart".[12] To the Corinthians he said that "The god of this age has blinded the minds of unbelievers, so that they

---

10 Colossians 3:23

11 Matthew 6:4

12 Romans 9:2

cannot see the light of the gospel"[13], thus giving us something concrete to think about when we pray for someone – that God would remove their blindness. Paul soon goes on to the great antidote to such discouragement – the multiplication principle: "All this is for your benefit, so that the grace that is reaching more and more people may cause thanksgiving to overflow to the glory of God."[14] Maybe this is why God allows us to see any fruit for our work at all – he knows we need all the encouragement we can get.

During the last term of my last year at Trinity College I was invited to a party thrown by a 'society girl' to celebrate the fact that she had recently become a Christian. I even remember some of the music! She played *Yesterday* by Lennon and McCartney and halfway through she stopped it and spoke into the silence, "I don't believe in yesterday any more!" Afterwards some of us said we would remember to pray for her and we did. I must admit my prayers fizzled out after a while – partly because I heard nothing more about her and partly because my faith got thin. I thought her home background might swamp her enthusiasm once she graduated.

Twenty-seven years later I was meeting a student at Heathrow Terminal Three and discovered he was also being met by his mother. We all drank sociable coffee once he had arrived and his mother and I chatted, compared notes and discovered we had attended Trinity at the same time. She said that it was unlikely that we would have ever met because, although she was now a missionary playing a key role in Bible translation in a sensitive part of the world, in those days she was a bit of a society girl who had just become a Christian. The same one! Why did God allow that chance meeting? Maybe to ensure I never lose heart. And maybe to remind me that, in the end, they are *his* disciples.

---

13 2 Corinthians 4:4
14 2 Corinthians 4:15

Growing your heart

Leading people is tiring. Paul said that "though outwardly we are wasting away, yet inwardly we are being renewed day by day."[15] The Holy Spirit reinforces us from the inside and God realises better than we do that it takes time for us to recharge our batteries. You cannot be God's gift to anyone as their leader if you are always tired and a shade below par. The Lord Jesus himself took time out with the disciples to be refreshed – it shows how human he was. This is what they were doing immediately before the feeding of the five thousand. "Because so many people were coming and going that they did not even have a chance to eat, he said to them, 'Come with me by yourselves to a quiet place and get some rest'."[16] The disciples not having "a chance to eat" wasn't a case of fasting, or choosing to skip lunch. There was simply more people-pressure than they could handle. They needed to retire from the fray every once in a while – and so do you. To set everybody's mind at ease it was Jesus who came up with the idea. Take time to think. Schedule it in. Try writing a diary or use your prayer diary. Read. There is constant popular pressure (which originates with the publishers) to read 'the latest.' This is simply the cult of the new, from which you may not learn much. Why not list the best books of the last 100 years and read them? Or the top 20 books of all time!

Other restful resources to use would be music and friends. Some leaders get so organised that by default they organise their friends out of their diary. Talking to (the right) friends can help to restore your soul. The world needs rested leaders.

Showing your heart

You may feel lovely thoughts in your heart about those you lead but, unless they discover this, your feelings may not do them

---

15 2 Corinthians 4:16

16 Mark 6:31

much good. Some New Testament leaders, far from being cold, unfeeling beings concerned only with principles, were able to fairly gush with emotion when the occasion called for it. How about, "It is right for me to feel this way about all of you, since I have you in my heart"?[17] When did you last write that to anybody?! Or, "What is our hope, our joy, or the crown in which we will glory in the presence of our Lord Jesus Christ when he comes? Is it not you? Indeed you are our glory and joy."[18] Paul wasn't beyond giving the Corinthians a regular outburst of emotion. After one of these intense self-disclosures he says, "Oh, our dear friends in Corinth, we are hiding nothing from you and our hearts are absolutely open to you. Any stiffness between us must be on your side, for we assure you there is none on ours. Do reward me (I talk to you as though you were my own children) with the same complete candour!"[19]

Paul had cracked the code of a communicating leader – showing your heart will stimulate others to show theirs and transform everybody's relationship to a deeper and more effective level. This doesn't mean that you need to 'go all emotional' on people, especially in some false way. For some of us it comes naturally to wear our heart on our sleeve. Others hope that a succession of winks and nods will suffice. Unfortunately it won't suffice. People are much more likely to misinterpret what you mean. If you are going to lead other people it is good to practise saying, "I feel." Here are some ground rules:

I feel

Can you hear the difference between "I feel so proud to belong to the body of Christ with you" and "You're great"? You put others at ease when you start off by saying. "I feel disappointed this evening after something you said," instead of, "You annoy

---

17 Philippians 1:7

18 1 Thessalonians 2:19,20

19 2 Corinthians 6:11-13 J.B. Phillips

me." The first is a statement about yourself, the second is about the other person and it immediately pins the blame on them. Even learning to express negative emotions clearly, when that is appropriate, is also a boost to communication because it clears the air. It is most effective to report how you feel now (rather than 10 days ago). Has God captured your heart on a particular project that you want others to be involved in? Show them your heart – as well as telling them the details.

Look behind you

Have you recently heard a new sound behind you as you walk the narrow road to follow Christ? When you look over your shoulder you might find friends who are trying to keep up with you because they want to follow him the way you do. Then you've become a leader.

The spread of God's Word across the world is not something he has left to chance. He has left it to people, normal Spirit-filled people. Because they are people he also calls leaders from among them to help the others reach their highest potential by serving them with a kingdom mentality. Such leaders don't work for the kudos they will get out of supervising others, but for the approval they will hear personally from the Lord of the harvest when they go to see him.

Knowing Christ and making him known to others is an adventure that will put significance into your day and destiny in your life. Wherever you live that life, your impact will have global implications as you bring forward God's agenda for the world. Only 100% dependence on the Holy Spirit will enable you to be the person God wants you to be, and your friends need you to be, day by day.

CHAPTER 10

TOOLED UP

In the chapters of *Sorted* I have sometimes referred to various resources which have helped me. The following list covers the same sort of subjects we have talked about in this book. It is simply a starting place. Many of the books listed have good bibliographies which will launch you into a lifetime of growth, spiritual challenge and stimulation.

About assurance of your relationship with Christ

- Philip Yancey, *What's So Amazing About Grace?* (Zondervan, 2002). For many people this is the book that has unlocked their understanding of how God loves us unconditionally.

Introducing Christian faith

- C.S. Lewis, *Mere Christianity* (Collins, 2012). Regarded by many as a classic statement of Christian faith, written by the author of the Narnia chronicles. The book started 70 years ago as transcripts of radio broadcasts, which makes for a conversational style of writing. It includes his celebrated argument for the deity of Christ.
- John Stott, *Basic Christianity* (IVP, 2008). A readable and logical explanation of how the gospel works which has had a world-wide circulation affecting the lives of thousands of people. A great book to give – or lend and follow up.
- *Knowing God Personally* (Agapé, 2006). This 20-page booklet is a read-along outline of the gospel that you can go through with someone else. It includes 11 key Bible passages suitably explained and accompanied with some diagrams, and an opportunity to respond.
- Nicky Gumbel, *Why Jesus?* (Alpha International, 1991). A well-designed inexpensive booklet intended for giving to a friend as a first introduction to following Jesus. Also comes in a similar format for Christmas: Why Christmas? (Alpha International, 2005)

- *JESUS* film on DVD (Agapé). An 80-minute version of the feature film Jesus, shot on location in Israel. It covers the birth, life, teaching, miracles, death and resurrection of Christ, using the text of Luke's gospel. Ending with a clear explanation of how to accept Christ with an on-screen opportunity to do so. The DVD is available in all the languages spoken by international visitors to Europe.

Advice about recommending Jesus to others

- Bill Bright, *Witnessing Without Fear: How to Share Your Faith with Confidence* (Thomas Nelson, 1993 from Agapé). Bill Bright was a towering example to me and many others in the area of personal witness and wrote copiously on the subject. This is a good summary book.
- *Living and Telling the Good News* (Agapé) – training course with leader's manual, course workbook and videos. Covers the same areas as *Sorted* with a wealth of practical ideas in the seminars.

Life in the workplace

- Mark Greene, *Thank God it's Monday* (Scripture Union, 2001). Combined in one book you get the rationale for excellence in work, how work glorifies God, how to maintain high standards of integrity at your work and how to bear witness to Christ in that environment. My wife and I bought a copy for each member of our team when this was published. We don't often do that.

Discipleship

- Robert Coleman, *The Masterplan of Evangelism* (Revell, 2006). Although you would think this book is about evangelism, and it is, Coleman also has much to say about

discipling others. This is a concise and biblical examination of what Jesus did to develop his disciples and the principles that flow out of this. For me it has been a coach on how to go about the whole discipling business.
- Walter Hendrichsen, *Disciples Are Made, Not Born* (David C Cook, 2002). This is like a teach-yourself-discipleship book. Nothing is left to the imagination, it is strongly based in the Bible and the wide extent of the author's practical experience shows clearly.

Answers to frequently asked questions

- *How to Turn Stumbling Blocks Into Stepping Stones* (Agapé, 2002). The idea here is that the best place to begin is the issue about which people have questions. There is a way to turn that very difficulty into a bridge to faith.
- Josh McDowell, *New Evidence That Demands a Verdict* (Thomas Nelson, 2010). This book has long since been a standard reference on the deity of Christ, the resurrection, the documents of the Bible and the predictions of the Old Testament.
- Josh McDowell, *More Than a Carpenter* (Authentic, 2011). This primer on the identity of Jesus and the evidence for his resurrection has sold more than 15 million copies. It lays out the facts of the case in a well researched and accessible format.
- Tim Keller, *The Reason for God* (Hodder & Stoughton, 2009). Keller moves with ease between references to popular culture and classical discussion of the existence of God. Always a good choice for giving or lending to a person new to the faith or outside of it altogether.
- Peter Kreeft & Roland Tacelli, *A Handbook of Christian Apologetics* (Ignatius, 2009). Treats all the major questions you are ever likely to hear with logic that can only be described as devastating.

- William Craig, *Reasonable Faith* (Crossway, 2008). A readable approach to questions of faith and reason. Excellent chapter on the resurrection which includes not only the historical evidence but also why that evidence is reliable.

Developing maturity

- Donald Whitney, *Spiritual Disciplines for the Christian Life* (NavPress, 2006). The most balanced book I know on this much-ignored aspect of Christian life – discipline. Draws on centuries of experience of devout Christians to give positive help in prayer, lifestyle, finance and many other issues of practical Christian living.
- Richard Foster, *Celebration of Discipline* (Hodder & Stoughton, 2008). Foster helpfully de-mystifies the whole spectrum of classical Christian disciplines like meditation, prayer and fasting, putting them within our reach.
- Gordon Fee & Douglas Stuart, *How to Read the Bible for All Its Worth* (Zondervan, 2003). For those of us who don't want to let others work out what we should believe. How to approach the various genres of writing included in the Bible and make the best of them.
- J.I. Packer, *Knowing God* (Hodder & Stoughton, 2005). Packer explains that this began when a magazine asked for "a series of articles on God angled for honest, no-nonsense readers who were fed up with facile Christian verbiage."
- A.W. Tozer, *The Pursuit of God* (Authentic, 2004). There are not many books published about God. This is one of the classics of our time. It is neither long nor complicated – just profound.
- Edith Schaeffer, *Affliction* (Paternoster, 1996). You won't get too far in life without having to think about adversity. Edith Schaeffer is one of few modern authors who helps you think through the issues biblically and honestly.

Christ's Great Commission

- Ralph Winter, *Perspectives on the World Christian Movement* (William Carey Library, 2009). This is not just a book – it's a compendium. It sits on my bookshelf right beside my desk. It has everything from William Carey's heart-felt appeal for missions in 1792 to the most recent analysis of where the world's 'people-groups' are distributed on earth today. Not only will it save you buying half a dozen other books, it includes specialist articles found nowhere else.
- Chris Wright, *The Mission of God* (IVP, 2006). Many books have been written on the Biblical theology of mission. It is hard to think of one that is so all-encompassing as this. Wright points out that mission is not just something you *find* in the Bible but a *basis for* the Bible.
- Elizabeth Elliot, *Shadow of the Almighty* (Harper and Row, 1990). Searingly honest, soaringly hopeful account of the spiritual growth of her beloved, Jim Elliott, who was to become her young missionary husband. He and his friends were then tragically martyred sparking a surge in 20th century missionary volunteers. I once went through a phase of reading only the Bible. This is the book that successfully tempted me to diversify a little.
- Jason Mandryk, *Operation World* (IVP USA, 2012). The subtitle is 'The Definitive Prayer Guide to Every Nation' – and it does exactly that. You can look up any nation in the world and find out who's doing what and how best to pray for the people who live there.

Biblical Leadership

- Henri Nouwen, *In the Name of Jesus* (Darton, Longman & Todd, 1989). Nouwen was someone who learned servant leadership, practised it and, eventually, quietly taught it. This is his definitive statement on the subject.

STUDY GUIDE

Chapter 1

1. Describe the 'life of destiny' that Jesus offers.
2. What is the first step into this life of destiny? What makes this step so important?
3. What 'cast-iron' promises form the basis for your relationship with Christ and your life of destiny?
4. John 1:12 tells us, "To all who received him, to those who believed in his name, he gave the right to become children of God." Revelation 3:20 says, "Here I am! I stand at the door and knock. If anyone hears my voice and opens the door, I will come in and eat with him and he with me." What are the promises in these verses? How do we claim them?
5. What role do feelings play in your relationship with Christ? How and when can feelings be misleading?
6. Some people are reluctant to step out into the life of destiny that Jesus offers because they are afraid of God's plan for their life. Have you ever felt this way? Discuss?

Reflection: Look back at the verses in question 4 above. Have you claimed these promises in John 1:12 and Revelation 3:20 for your own life?

Action: Can you think of someone that God has placed in your path with whom you could share the story of his love? Discuss with a friend how best to talk to that person and pray together for them.

Chapter 2

1. Why do many believers today feel unable or not so inclined to make an impact on the world around them?
2. This chapter is entitled 'Impact of Forgiveness'. How does God's forgiveness impact our daily lives?
3. Why would some Christians tend to exert so much energy 'pedalling harder' to prove themselves to God?
4. Which of our sins will God forgive? Past? Present? Future?
5. Describe the three kinds of person Paul outlines in 1 Corinthians 2:14-3:3.
6. What does it mean to 'confess'? How is confessing like breathing out?
7. What happens when we don't confess? Does it affect our eternal relationship with God? How does it affect our daily fellowship with God?
8. Why is it important to be sure about God's forgiveness?

Reflection & Action: Review the paragraph entitled 'Action points', and spend some time working through the six steps mentioned, applying John 1:9 to your own life now.

Chapter 3

1. When Jesus left his disciples, what one thing were they lacking in order to carry out their special life assignment? How are we similar to those disciples? How are we different?
2. When Jesus was preparing to leave, why did he spend so much time talking about the Holy Spirit?
3. In John chapters 14 to 16, what is Jesus' rationale for saying that we would be better off here without him?
4. Who is the Holy Spirit and why did he come?
5. What does it mean to be filled with the Holy Spirit? Is this just a suggestion for believers?
6. Why are many believers not filled with the Holy Spirit?
7. How is being filled with the Holy Spirit like breathing in?
8. In Ephesians 5:18 God gives us a command, and in 1 John 5:14-15 he gives us a promise. What is the command? What is the promise? How do these relate to being filled with the Holy Spirit?
9. What does it look like in everyday life to be filled with the Spirit?

Reflection: Reflect on God's command and promise in Ephesians 5:18 and 1 John 5:14-15.

Action: By faith, ask God to fill you with the Holy Spirit. Then thank him for doing so.

Chapter 4

1. Why do you think the New Testament writers preferred to use the word 'walking' to describe our life in Christ?
2. Why is 'spiritual breathing' important for the believer?
3. What does a life of 'walking in the light' look like? What might it look like for a believer who doesn't walk in the light?
4. According to Acts 1:8, what is the connection between the Spirit and being a witness?
5. Is it possible to 'keep in step with the Spirit' from moment to moment? How can this get derailed?
6. Thinking about the recent past, were there any times when you were 'out of step' with the Spirit? What were some of the causes?
7. What are some of your resources as a child of God?
8. If the Holy Spirit is like the *oxygen* for our life, what is our life's *food*?
9. What is so radical about prayer?
10. As Spirit-filled people, how are we all called to be ambassadors? How seriously do you take this calling?

Reflection: Spend some time meditating on 2 Corinthians 5:17-21. Think particularly about what this says about your identity in Christ and your appointment as an ambassador.

Action: Starting now, breathe out (confess) and breathe in (be filled with the Spirit), and make it a point to practise spiritual breathing daily.

Chapter 5

1. This chapter begins by describing the war zone we live in as believers. Describe the enemies we face in this battle.
2. The Bible says temptation comes from the world, the flesh, and the devil. How do these sources reveal themselves?
3. What does it mean to have your 'emotional home' in a godless world? What are the problems with that?
4. What are the two opposing influences working in the life of a believer? How do they conflict with one other?
5. What does C.S. Lewis outline as Satan's two basic strategies? How is the believer able to resist these strategies?
6. What is involved in living by faith? How would that work out in your life?
7. Relate an instance in your life in which you were especially aware that God supplied your needs. How did you thank him?
8. When was the last time you demonstrated faith by thanking God in difficult or trying circumstances?

Reflection: Think of some practical ways to develop the habit of praising God. How is that habit beneficial to a person's life?

Action: Think of some things that cause you anxiety or distress and apply 1 Thessalonians 5:18 – "Give thanks in all circumstances, for this is God's will for you in Christ Jesus."

Chapter 6

1. Who recommended Christ to you? How did that happen?.
2. Who do you think would be the first people to whom you should recommend Christ?
3. If you are consistently walking in the Spirit, your friends will notice that you are different. Can they identify your differentness as having something to do with following Jesus? Have you ever spoken to them about it?
4. What is the connection between Christian maturity and witnessing?
5. What are some of the essential steps to take as we prepare to recommend Jesus to others?
6. Why is being prepared important to recommending Jesus to others?
7. What is so powerful about articulating your own story?
8. What do you think are the most basic things a person needs to know in order to make an informed decision to follow Christ? What is the importance of having an outline of these things?

Reflection: Take some time to remember your own journey from unbelief to belief. Thank God for your journey. Reflect on some of the changes that have come about in your life since making a decision to follow Jesus.

Action: Work through the four 'straight story' questions, writing out short answers to each of them, and practise telling them to a friend. 1. What was your attitude before you took Christ seriously? 2. Why did you begin to take Christ seriously? 3. How did you say "Yes" to Christ? 4. What difference does following Christ make in your life?

Chapter 7

1. What word is common to these instructions of Jesus to the disciples: "Go and make disciples..." (Matthew 28:19); "Go into all the world..." (Mark 16:15); "...go and bear fruit." (John 15:16)? What are the implications?
2. Does Jesus' challenge to take the initiative apply only to missionaries? If not, who is the challenge for?
3. What are the three 'sonic booms' that you need to be aware of when you take the initiative to talk to people about Christ?
4. Can you differentiate between a conversation about religion and a conversation about Jesus?
5. What is meant by the comment: "You haven't really communicated the gospel message completely until the question has been popped"? Do you agree or disagree?
6. What possible impact could it have on your relationship with somebody if you were to talk to them about Christ? What's the worst case scenario? What's the best case scenario?
7. You have read the statement, "success in sharing your faith is simply taking the initiative to talk about Jesus Christ in the power of the Holy Spirit and leaving the results to God." How can this statement can be a source of encouragement to you? If you talk to someone in the power of the Holy Spirit and that person does not receive Christ, why should you call that a 'success'?
8. What is the idea behind 'spiritual multiplication'? Explain how this is different from addition.
9. What is the recipe for spiritual growth that Paul passes on to Timothy? (Hint: 2 Timothy 2:2)

Reflection: In the previous chapter we discussed how it is just as important to talk to God about people as it is to talk to people about God. Take some time to pray about people you know who need to hear about Christ's love for them.

Action: Come up with a list of your 'Five in Focus'. Think about people in your sphere of influence: people you work with, study with, play with and live with (it might be good to write this in a chart with those four columns). Choose five people from your chart for whom you would like to pray. Ask God to show you the first steps to take with each of them.

Chapter 8

1. Why do you think God wants us to be involved in his global enterprise of spreading the gospel message?
2. What indications do we have from the Scriptures about God's love for lost people?
3. What is the Great Commission?
4. Who gave the Great Commission? To whom was it given? Is it for us or just the first disciples?
5. What is God's 'Plan A' for expressing his love and forgiveness to the world? What is his 'Plan B'?
6. Where do we derive our right to talk to people about Christ?
7. What all is involved in the Great Commission?
8. Where does the Great Commission apply?
9. What is meant when the Bible talks about 'nations'?
10. What's already been done in the Great Commission? What's left to do in the Great Commission?
11. What are three valuable areas of training for someone wanting to get involved in cross-cultural mission?

Reflection: Take some time to think and pray about the 'people group(s)' in which God has placed you? What would it take for everyone of those people to have a chance to hear how to come to know God personally?

Action: How will the Great Commission affect your diary for the next 12 months? Plan some changes to reflect this.

Chapter 9

1. How is a chapter on leadership relevant reading for all believers?
2. How does the world see leadership differently from the way Jesus saw it in Luke 22 and Matthew 23?
3. What's the link between being a leader and being a servant?
4. What are some of the different leadership roles a person can take on?
5. What are some of the tell-tale weaknesses that show up when leadership has gone wrong?
6. What are your thoughts about the comment: "leaders have more faults than others because they have more, not less, temptation"?
7. Describe the principle of the 'audience of One'.

Reflection: Take some time to reflect on who your 'audience' is.

Action: Draw up a simple plan for personal growth. Look at the different leadership roles (direction-setter, change agent, coach, spokesperson and steward), and make some goals for one or two areas in which you'd like to grow. Your goals need to be measurable and attainable. Ask someone you trust to hold you accountable. Make sure that regular rest gets scheduled in as well.